THE BOY DAVID

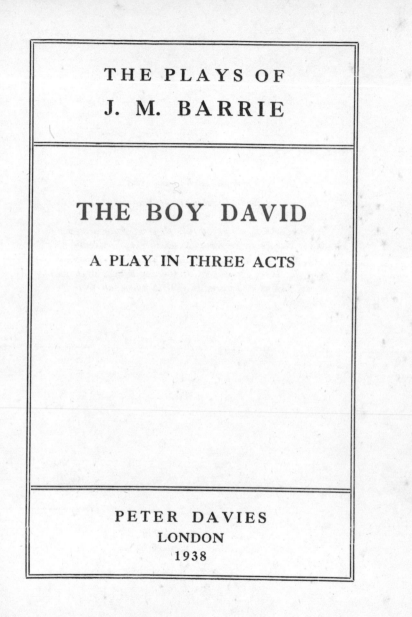

THE PLAYS OF
J. M. BARRIE

THE BOY DAVID

A PLAY IN THREE ACTS

PETER DAVIES
LONDON
1938

Published in January 1938

Copyright and all rights reserved

Printed in Great Britain for PETER DAVIES LTD.
by T. and A. CONSTABLE LTD. at the University Press, Edinburgh.

CONTENTS

CAST OF "THE BOY DAVID"

As produced at His Majesty's Theatre, London,
on 14th December 1936

Characters nearly in the order of their appearance

Jesse		WILSON COLEMAN
The Wife of Jesse . . .		JEAN CADELL
Eliab		BASIL C. LANGTON
Amnon	Sons	PETER BULL
Aminadab	of	ERIC ELLIOTT
Shammah	Jesse	ROBERT EDDISON
David		ELISABETH BERGNER
The Prophet Samuel . . .		JOHN MARTIN-HARVEY
Jonathan (Son of Saul) . . .		BOBBY RIETTI
Ophir (a Captain in the Army of Saul)		LEON QUARTERMAINE
Saul (King of Israel) . . .		GODFREY TEARLE
A Guard		WILLIAM D'ARCY
Nathan when young . . .		ION SWINLEY
Abner (Captain of the Slingers) .		JOHN BOXER
The Armour-Bearer of Goliath .		ELLIS IRVING
The Woman of Endor . . .		MARGARET CHATWIN

———

Slingers of Israel and Philistines

———

Presented by CHARLES B. COCHRAN
Scenery and Costumes by AUGUSTUS JOHN and ERNST STERN
Music by WILLIAM WALTON
The play directed by KOMISARJEVSKY

vi

PREFACE

' IT is the play he might have written before
ever he left Scotland, had he known how. The
Boy David keeps his sheep upon the hills round
Kirriemuir. . . .'

With it then, if this be so, the wheel of his
career comes, in a sense, full circle. It was the
work of his old age—if nowadays at seventy-six
a man is old—and during the fifteen preceding
years he had written nothing of importance.[1]
The play's popular welcome might have satisfied
many a dramatist. But he had had his fill of
such success in the past. Its critical reception,
expressed and implicit, disappointed him, even
grievously ; and the more so since illness had
kept him from rehearsals, robbing him of his
chance to make the final additions and adjust-

[1] For the theatre. But if faultless taste, unerring skill,
and the apparent ease which is the reward of much past
winnowing labour of mind and pen, make for importance in
literature, the privately printed, recently published *The
Greenwood Hat* and a short story, *Farewell, Miss Julie Logan*,
are important enough.

ments, upon which, in his nicely calculated art, so much depended. Up to that point he had given of his best, and—secretly diffident as he could be about his work, and scrupulously, even harshly, critical—he thought it good, and that all promised well. He made no open complaint about the result; that was not his way. But the grief struck the deeper. There the personal aspect of the matter may be left.

The play is now given to the reader; given to him, moreover, exactly as it was to the producer and actors, as material for them to work upon. And, to appreciate the art and the craft of it, the reader must try to put himself in their place. Barrie was already an accomplished writer of essays and novels when he first gave his mind at all seriously to the theatre. Having done so, he set to work painstakingly to learn its craft, not presuming in the least upon the earlier achievement. He wrote, indeed, no more novels. There was much ado in those days about the craft of letters. Stevenson had been proud of his craftsmanship; Kipling was so; and Barrie, besides this, was, where work was concerned, the most practical of men. He had not served his apprenticeship as a Nottingham journalist in vain. He turned out articles of the required length for Greenwood's *St. James's Gazette*, and his novels were of marketable size. The more he was to be his own master in other respects, the more individual the work itself, the better it would be to conform to the common rule in less essential things. Nor was this worldly wisdom only. There was respect in it for other men's crafts : the editor's, the publisher's, the bookseller's. There was also a sense of the need for some such ballast to his own capricious imagination. His Pegasus went better in harness.

So he set himself to master in its turn the craft of the theatre, and very deft at it he soon became. Into the dominant dramatic movement of the time he did not, as it happened, fit very well. Realism was in the ascendant, and to try poetry or fantasy was to risk being labelled amateur or crank. Had the theatre he found been the theatre of to-day, with its many technical freedoms since won—the revived equivalent of the Elizabethan stage, its anachronisms reconceded ; the spirit of the Masque and the Dance alive again and welcome invaders—he was the man of all others to have profited by them. It was just such a theatre that he needed. Too much to expect him, coming to the craft as a man of letters, an outsider, to create one. To be practical he had to take the theatre as he found it. So he mastered its ways and did well enough in them, and often asked no more of it than it knew how to give him. Yet, to do his best and be most himself, he knew that he wanted something more and something different ; and his dramatic progress is marked by efforts to gain it. He never attained to the full freedom he needed ; he went on as he had begun, his fancies wedded—and at times incongruously—to a realism of method. But he helped win it for others. The English theatre to-day owes much to the encouraging influence of Barrie's originality.

Once sure enough of his dramatist's share of the craft, he delighted to set his fellow-craftsmen in the theatre experimenting, to have its complex machinery made to do for him what it did for nobody else. *Peter Pan* was an achievement in this alone. Its amusing technical tricks may pass unremarked now, since changes have been rung on them in other plays for a generation past. But before its first production there must have been much misgiving, much wondering among all concerned, from manager and actors to stage-hands and call-boy, whether this or that novel ' effect ' could possibly ' come off.' And a tribute of remembrance is due to Dion Boucicault, thanks largely to whose patient ingenuity they all did. Nor should this aspect of the play be decried. *Peter Pan* is a masque—The Masque of Adventurous Childhood, we might call it—and scenery and machinery are therefore an integral part of it.

Painting and carpentry are the soul of masque . . .

the *soul* they should not be ; but it was only that usurpation which drew Jonson's sarcasm, he had given due credit to Inigo Jones till then.

Barrie could court and meet with failures in this kind. A political satire called *Josephine*—too trivial in itself besides—collapsed under them. He grew expert at compromise. There is much of the masque in *A Kiss for Cinderella* ; but not enough machinery to de-humanise it. The magic in *Dear Brutus* involves none at all, and the more realistically the play is treated the better. But in *Mary Rose* the real and the unreal are boldly mingled ; there is neither evasion of the difficulty nor compromise. Upon

the magic island she must disappear before our
eyes.   This is matter for a single risky moment,
which is, moreover, led up to with extraordinary
dramatic skill, and a sympathetic producer may
compass it.   But what of the last scene, between
the ghost of her, never grown old, and her lost
son, unrecognised in the rough Anzac soldier,
who, after all the nice, cultured people in the
play, with their sentimental memories and
regrets, have failed to face the challenge of her
return, unchanged, from among the dead, sees,
he alone, that oblivion and annihilation is the
single mercy left ?   Apart from the problem of a
setting in realistic scenery, how is the poignantly
tragic beauty of the scene, its metaphysic and
the essential poetry of its idea, how are these
things to be expressed in the workaday language,
the familiar action of dramatic realism ?

It is but one—if an extreme—example of
the problem that Barrie was continually challenging himself to solve : how to wed fancy
and poetry to the actualities of his realistic
modern stage ; how, in fact, to make the best
of two dramatic worlds.   And not till his plays
are examined from this point of view is it to be
seen how much ingenuity, tact and judgment

go to the solving. Given the admitted make-believe of a *Peter Pan*, there is no great difficulty, the dramatist may lead us along what fantastic ways he will. But if he wants to win us to that self-forgetful belief in the fiction of his play, under which alone the theatre may exercise its full spell on us, then it will be safer for him to choose the most commonly accepted convention, and, having chosen it, by all means to abide in it, not to try playing fast and loose between one sphere of illusion and another. It was this spell, to be nightly cast upon the great uncritical public, that he wanted to wield. So he accepted the popular convention ; never thought, probably, of doing otherwise. If this did not suffice him he must enlarge it, but without changing it. Rejecting it, he might perhaps, after a failure or so, have evolved some other. But he would hardly have considered this a ' practical ' proceeding, nor the drama resulting ' real drama ' ; he might even have seen something a little arrogant in the attempt. And so it came to his committing himself to the solving of one very nearly insoluble dramatic problem after another.

The difficulties in *Mary Rose* are probably to

be overcome.   Those of *The Boy David* wear a
different aspect, and Barrie makes one formidable
addition to them.   Machinery there is none to
count, but for the scenes of the visions in the
last Act.[1]   Over these, with a comradely candour,
he throws himself on his producer's mercy :

>   *All this calls for adroitness from stage experts*
>   *that is beyond the author's skill, who knows what*
>   *he wants but not how to get it and has now given*
>   *them enough to ponder over for one day.* . . .

Such stage directions would not ordinarily have
survived for publication.   But this gives us in
a few strokes his workmanlike attitude towards
the theatre and his view of his own place there.
And the directions to the actors, constantly recur-
ring, with their careful explanations of why and
wherefore and their warnings against one error
or another, show that so far, certainly, he
both knew what he wanted and, at any rate,
how it would *not* be got.   Their survival may
now help to set the reader acting the play in
his own mind—for so every reader of a play
should do—as Barrie meant it to be acted.   He

[1] The actual appearance of Goliath, which did involve a
little stage trickery, was abandoned after a few trial per-
formances.

will not find it, even under such uncritical
conditions, to be quite so easy a task as it may
appear ; and the attempt may teach him, among
other things, that the perfect simplicity so re-
peatedly demanded is not a very simple thing
for actors to achieve.

The formidable addition to his usual difficulties
is, of course, that he takes a known story to
dramatize. He has at once lost a large part of
his liberty—more valuable to him than to most
—to adapt character to event and event to
character, and both to an imaginative scheme
which may grow and change. He has lost the
benefits of surprise ; we know what is to come.
Finally, it is a story from the Bible, and one
told and retold to us in childhood, and so durably
illustrated in our own memories that any re-
shaping or recolouring of it is likely to set us
resentfully on the defensive. Yet it must now
be enlarged upon, and rewritten besides into
dialogue and the present tense. And when it
comes to that, why, he is laying his hand also
upon the very Ark of the Literary Covenant.

Of this last part of the problem there can be
no impeccable solution. The Bible, it is true,
largely records the spoken word, and our

translation of it was meant to be read aloud.
Much of it declaims well, and the Song of
Solomon is actually a dialogue. Peele, in his
David and Bethsabe, paraphrased whole passages
into blank verse, more faithfully than Sternhold
and Hopkins had put the Psalms into rhyme,
giving, one may suppose — though now in
England, yet still not in Scotland, we have
changed our minds about this—as little general
offence. And is, indeed,

> Thus Nathan saith unto his Lord the King :
> There were two men, both dwellers in one towne,
> And one was mighty and exceeding rich
> In oxen, sheepe and cattell of the field,
> The other poore having no oxe nor calfe
> Nor other cattell save one little Lamb . . .

an unpardonable treason to its original ? But,
if for need of matter only, Peele could not stop
at this. He is following the story faithfully,
step by step, and he must also, he takes it,
provide his actors with a continuous flow of
narrative and rhetoric combined. So David
expatiates upon his sins and the child's death,
and again upon Absalom's death, Bethsabe too ;
and the Bible's fine reticence is, we may well
feel, fatally compromised.

Here, nevertheless, may have been for Peele the best means to his end in that theatre with that audience. And a pretty counterfeit of it, however misplaced in ours, would doubtless win praise to-day from sophisticated amateurs of this sort of thing. But Barrie has his own theatre and his own audience exclusively in mind. And he will not take refuge, even there, in the conventions, worn to commonplace, by which such themes and characters are commonly magnified to heroic size—and distorted and de-humanised in the process. His David and Saul and Samuel are to be made as actual to us as people we pass in the street, their thoughts and feelings given the currency of our own. Yet something of their legendary status and its glamour must be left them; we shall pay no deference to their familiar names alone. It is the dealing with this that replaces in the problem the difficulties with those projections of his own fancy, which he has more or less learnt to render into terms of realism. But realism alone will not do for him now. These figures must be realised and be left rarefied too. It is no easy task.

Nor will the least troublesome part of it be the question of the sort of speech to put in their

b

mouths.   Barrie has to make the best he can of
both worlds in this too.   All dramatic speech
must be economised within some convention.
The realistic writer tries to make us forget it.
But an accepted means of persuading us that
those actors we see and hear are Kings in
Babylon or Vikings old is to set them talking
in an unusual way.   And something of the sort
would seem to be needed.   In the one case the
liker a character to anybody we know the
greater the illusion ; in the other, the less.   The
speech in *The Boy David* is a compromise ;
simple enough in vocabulary to set us at ease
with the characters ; removed from reality by
a mixture of Scottish locutions with a few
inversions and redundancies ; given a recurrent
dignity by echoes of scriptural phrase.   Under
literary analysis it may show up badly, but in
its speaking must be the test.   Even here a

> Noble captain, your fame grows apace . . .

may ring hollow, and a

> Thus also did I do . . .

prove feeble.   And the play's auxiliary passages
do move rather wordily and even woodenly
along.   (Were they more conventionally done,

they might be worse written and sound better, to the lay ear at least. Blank verse or pompous prose are still the accepted buckram for this use.) But where the characters are alive, as if in their own right, the vitality of the matter clarifies the form.

Take the scene of David's encounter on his way to the camp with the unknown Saul:

SAUL (*roughly*). You seem to be a country boy. Who are you? What do you here?

DAVID (*rather frightened*). I am David, son of Jesse.

SAUL. I know no Jesse.

DAVID. I did but halt to ask you how I may get me to the camp of Saul. My father is of Bethlehem, and there I do tend his sheep in the fields.

SAUL. Sheep? Ay, truly, I see them in your eyes.

DAVID (*disturbed*). Do you?

SAUL (*who sees that he is being taken literally*). And I hear the sheep-bells in your voice.

DAVID (*fearing that there must be something wrong with himself*). Can it be so?

SAUL. Sheep! I too, boy, have led the sheep home, as many times as there are stones upon the road to Jericho. I was a shepherd—once—myself.

DAVID. Were you? You do not look so now. What is your name?

SAUL (*introducing them with a touch of humour*). Son of Jesse, I am—the son of Kish. (DAVID *bows*.)

DAVID. Was your land fat or lean?

SAUL. Here and there were fat parcels of ground—but the barren places, David! (*He begins to be amused by* DAVID.)

DAVID (*sympathetically*). I know! How I know! And the goats in the barren places— waiting to pounce if one blade springs up. How many sheep had you?

SAUL. Five hundred, it may be, when I returned from a fray.

DAVID (*astounded*). Five hundred! No! And kine?

SAUL. I forget how many.

DAVID (*scandalised*). *Forget* how many!

SAUL (*seating himself and speaking with apparent gravity*). Listen and direct your ways. I had two camels and an olive press, and my well was bricked.

DAVID (*gasping*). Bricked! (*Boasting*) Nevertheless there is no water like to the Well of Bethlehem which is by the gate.

SAUL. That may be so, but I had a fig-tree that bore twice in the year.

DAVID (*who stands near him with legs wide apart and head thrust forward—impressed*). Truly you were in a big way!

—and so on; Saul forgetting present cares and the future's threats in his delight in the boy (in whom, as we know, but as he does not, those very threats are embodied; the tonic irony, this, which gives edge to the scene), and in the memories of his own boyhood, till the two are fast friends, and he

> . . . *puts a hand on* DAVID'S *shoulder and walks him back and forward.*
>
> DAVID. My mother made my coat.
>
> SAUL. *My* mother, I do remember, used to make mine!
>
> DAVID (*finding this a remarkable coincidence*). Did she? We are very like each other, Shepherd.
>
> SAUL. The likeness between us grows every moment! Did your mother also make your harp? . . .
>
> DAVID. Oh no. My father did want to belt me for having a harp, but my mother dissuaded him.
>
> SAUL. A good, but perhaps weak mother.
>
> DAVID. She is not weak! She will let none belt me but herself. (*Standing up for her*) There is in all Bethlehem no woman who can lay on as my mother does.

Here, at least, is neither flat realism nor obtrusive artifice. And no reader, surely, who has any sense for dramatic dialogue, can fail to appreciate its art; the masterly economy, the equilibrium, the resiliency of it all. Every speech has its motive, and contributes besides to the advancing

of the scene or the unfolding of the character,
with a continuity as clear as a good drawing or
a line of pure melody. It is fecund dialogue. It
sows seeds in the actor's imagination. It does
not shackle him. He can fulfil its obligations
without effort, and inhabit the character at his
ease. Other dramatists cultivate other qualities ;
a richness of texture into which may be woven
profounder emotion, more intricate thought, or
less persuasiveness with more command. But
in the delicacy and clarity of such an exchange
as this, with its invitation to the actors of it to
respond in kind, above all, in the ungrudging
freedom of opportunity it offers them—that
peculiar self-abnegation, the dramatist's last
secret ; by many never learnt—Barrie is surely
unsurpassed.

Nor is he easily to be bettered in the concision
with which he can make character and situation
eloquent each of the other. David comes riding
on his ass into the line of battle and to within
challenging distance of Goliath. He is ' exalted,'
as he terms it ; the Spirit of the Lord is upon
him. There is no descriptive expatiating upon
this, no loss of actuality, therefore. The wonder
of it is prosaically reflected in the suspicious

astonishment with which the soldiers greet him, and translated, with David himself—as everything in the play is made 'real'—into the rapt, inspired innocence of youth. The bustle and disputing obscure him for a moment, and then reveal him sitting by the brook quietly gathering pebbles for his sling, while he puts it to Jonathan:

> . . . they say that he who kills Goliath acquires his tent and his spear. . . . I fear not to sleep in his tent if there is a lamp. But his spear! If his spear is like unto a weaver's beam, as they say, how shall I be able to carry it on my shoulder?

Is that all, he is asked, he can think of at such a moment? And he answers, with boyish preciseness:

> It is chiefly that.

The fears of the rest for him infect him a little. When the challenge must be blown on the horn and he is asked if even now he is not afraid, he answers:

> Perhaps I am afraid—but thus does David.

—and he blows it. At his sight of Goliath:

> He is of a size even more huge than they said. Jonathan, I am not *quite* sure now that I shall win.

But he will not run away. Then we hear the
voice of the giant :

    GOLIATH. Now shall Israel be shamed for
mocking me with such a champion. Look, insect,
upon Goliath of Gath.
    DAVID. Lo, I have looked and you are smaller
than they said.
    GOLIATH. How many pebbles, little one, are in
your wallet ?
    DAVID. There are five, but I think I shall not
need them all. . . .

It is in David's speech, its strict simplicity
tempered by an occasional odd turn, coloured
by an unexpected word or so, that the vital
medium needed is hit upon ; and it commonly
evokes as vital a response. The very life of the
play, indeed, radiates from David, and the whole
body of it is made to fit round him—to fit, that
is to say, this particular David of Barrie's
imagining.

He is demonstrably, by weight and measure,
not the David of the Bible ; and the ' Boy ' of
the play's title warns us that he is not meant
to be. Not that the Bible itself is consistent in
its early descriptions of him ; upon one page
he is ' a mighty valiant man, and a man of war,'

and upon another a 'youth' and a 'stripling,' not of fighting age, since his brothers scold him for having come in the naughtiness of his heart to see the battle. But Barrie is not transcribing a chronicle. He is taking an old tale for a theme, interpreting it anew, treating it as a parable for the expression of the idea that he finds in it, readjusting it for the better expression of the idea. He has good exemplars, were there need of them, in the Greek dramatists, who treated their heroic tales in much the same way. And must this one not be treated so merely because it comes from the Bible? Those to whom the Bible is a living thing have never accorded it that frigid respect—a sceptic offspring, rather, of the Higher Criticism! Their homage is to something more than accuracy, their tribute to translate the text of it yet again into the terms of their own lives for the proving of its verities there. Barrie, in his boyhood, was taught to look upon it so; in this last piece of work the man he has become applies the lesson after his own fashion.

The theme which he extracts for his play from the Biblical story is embodied in the conflict between David and Saul. And many of life's conflicts are reflected in it ; between youth and age, good luck and ill, between the strength of innocence and the weakening doubt which knowledge brings, and, worst of all, conflict not between those who hate, but those who love each other, forced on them by an overriding fate, kindling conflict within themselves too, and so doubly bitter. If he amends the story it is to give fuller significance to the theme. David becomes all but a child, so that he may strangle the lion and the bear and overcome the Philistine by no possible strength of his own (though — never to lose touch with reality — it *is* just possible for a stone from a boy's sling to slay a giant), but because the Spirit of the Lord is upon him. He is secretly anointed by Samuel (not, as in the story, ' in the midst of his brethren '), and we see age prostrate itself before divinely gifted youth. In his innocence he tells Saul the secret, launching the javelin at his own heart ; he conspires against God's will of him in vain. The wary Saul seeks everywhere for the threatened danger to his throne, except in the insignificance of that passing shepherd-boy—though he, too, was just such a shepherd-boy once. He even unbars the way for him to do the deed which is to be his own undoing. The secret out, is not his downfall only the more certainly destined if the God who deserts him can make this confiding child its instrument ? He could kill him. Though he now loves him, he tries to kill him, and will degrade and embitter the rest of his life by trying. But he cannot kill him. It is one of life's fundamental conflicts that is here reduced to such deceptively simple terms and crystallised, as drama should be, into significant action and a few revealing words.

The marvel of the boy David is flashed on us at our very first sight of him, bursting in and discharging that ' glorious mouthful ' :

Mother, I have killed a lion !

—in the very contrast between the looks of him and the preposterous statement. Remark too the nice art of that initial ' Mother.' It tells the actor just how to speak the line, is his keynote for the whole scene to come. Remark how the cold water of mere common sense, the ridicule and supperless punishment to follow, erode even David's own belief in what he has done till Samuel's unwitting witness establishes the truth of it. Then the marvel is epitomised in the boy's appeal to him :

> Do you think you could get my mother to give me my milk as I am he who killed the lion and the bear ?

To which Samuel—who, as a prophet, is not to be astonished by the Lord's doings—responds with an authoritative demand for

His milk.

The secret of the anointing is broken to Saul, and its consequences accumulate in just such another combination of action and speech, when David—proud of the accomplishment—prostrates himself before him upon learning that this shepherd man is the King. Then follows :

SAUL. Tell me, David, how did you know about prostrating ?

DAVID. Behold, there was an old man I did see do it.

SAUL. To a king ?

DAVID (*merry at the thought*). No ! (*He tells his cause of merriment*) Saul, he did it to me !

SAUL (*gripping him*). Be still, boy. This old man—how looked he ?

DAVID. A poor one, but kind. He said he was a prophet.

SAUL. Did he say his name?

DAVID. He was called Samuel. . . . It was in our house at Bethlehem, and he was secret. He carried a wallet and in it a horn, and he prayed and wetted my head with wet from the horn. And when he was going away he did prostrate himself—before David! (*He laughs at it.*)

Saul's sentence, from the boy's unknowing lips. David's too?

SAUL (*putting a sorrowful hand on* DAVID'S *head*). Thou doomed boy.

DAVID (*bewildered*). Doomed? Am I doomed, Saul?

SAUL. One of us two friends is doomed.

DAVID (*startled, very childlike*). Do you not like me now?

SAUL (*mournfully*). I like you well. . . .

David turns, happily reassured, to his harp, while Saul broods apart.

SAUL (*at last, speaking tragically*). There is an enemy in my habitation.

DAVID. An enemy? If it is so, kill him, Saul, kill him. (*He continues to play.*)

SAUL (*after a pause*). I will kill him. David, it is you I am to kill.

DAVID (*looking up and smiling happily*). Oh no, son of Kish! (*But seeing* SAUL'S *face, he rises and draws back. . . .*)

Are not these scenes, in their directness and allusiveness, simplicity and complexity combined, samples of a true and very fine dramatic art ?

There is the contrast between the respondings of the two—of the man once chosen now rejected, and of youth newly elect—to the ways of the Lord with them. There is the likeness in the contrast besides. Again, to bring the matter home to us, we are lent spectacles—Barrie's own inevitably—to read it by. Saul's answer to the sentence passed on him by God through his Prophet is given in the scene with the young Nathan, he who will return one day to reproach King David for his sins. Its theology reflects that half-emancipated typically nineteenth-century position, by which a man will have no mediating priest stand between him and his God—even though it be a god he only dreads and in his heart condemns. Half a faith is not better than none. But is not this a quite appropriate enlarging of the mind of the God-deserted Saul ?

David finds a more elusive god in the mysterious ' Other One,' on whom he learns to call to inspire and ' exalt ' him. This is the god of every man of genius, who builds better than he knows how to build, now thankfully adored, the god of ' Non nobis, Domine . . .', and next denied :

> I, David, son of Jesse, am the one who slew Goliath, and none helped me, for I did it alone . . . and that is false, for He helped me. . . . It was His pebble. . . . 'Twas also He who slew the lion and the bear . . . (*with a cry*) I want to do something all by myself.

For if he cannot, something tells him, the time may come when he also will find himself deserted by his God, and no better than an ordinary man.

The planning of the play's last Act must have puzzled Barrie not a little. The simplest way would have been to round off the story neatly, as an episode in David's youth. But then its true significance would have been lost. Such wonders are only to be wrought as a prelude to greater things. So we have the hardy device of the visions of what is to come. They fit, we may remark, into the very latest scientific speculations upon the nature of time. Yet this kind of play had better be rounded into a certain convincing unity of time and space. So we are given the final 'pastoral' scene of David guarding his sheep. We leave him as we found him, save for his trophy, for Goliath's spear, which he drags from its hiding-place as the curtain falls. And—the 'Other One' not helping him, as he has dared half-defiantly, half-apprehensively to say—he *can* already carry it on his shoulder. Nor does this quiet epilogue lack significance. Read it in the light of the last vision, the scene between the ghosts of Samuel and Saul. In their limbo they have forgotten that they were Prophet and King. The one remembers only that his sons were a trouble to him, the other that he once went on a journey to seek his father's asses which had strayed. If not in life, then in death, the wheel comes full circle, and the great things are no greater than the small.

H. G.-B.

ACT I

ACT I

THE HOUSE OF JESSE IN BETHLEHEM

The Scene of Act I is in Bethlehem, and is the dwelling-house of Jesse, a small farmer. The time is about three thousand years ago. The action of the play is almost continuous.

Bethlehem (of which in Act I we see only this room) was a small place in those days, but of a certain importance chiefly for its wool. It was on a hill, protected from enemies by a stout stone wall, and beneath it were the sheep-fields. Jesse's home, like its neighbours, was a one-storey flat-roofed building of stone and bricks which were made of mud. It had an earthen floor in which no doubt his domestic animals scraped for sustenance. This room, which to modern eyes would seem less inviting than the living-room of an agricultural labourer to-day, is strikingly bare of furniture such as to us seem necessities, though there is no real poverty. There are no tables or chairs. There is no carpet, everybody sits on the floor. Here and there are sheep-skins and goat-skins. The ceiling must be as low as possible and the room as small as the exigencies of the stage allow. This is important, as it is to be an intimate scene. The ceiling is raftered and there are some lower rafters on which agricultural implements, sheep-pelts, etc., are obviously stowed away. From the rafters hang a few smoked haunches of mutton and beef. The fire is in the middle of the room. This fire is a large open one of stone and sods sunk into the ground and surrounded by an irregular circle of clay. There is no chimney, and such smoke as there is travels up the walls into a smoky roof and has blackened them. The fire is alight and a big pot stands upon it. There are other culinary utensils near by, mostly of clay blackened by soot. There are two practical doors, namely the entrance up-stage on stage R and a door up-stage on L which leads (though they are not seen) to the store closets, the manger, and other important parts connected with the farmer's occupation. The entrance door is R up-stage, and is of wood and hard mud and sunk deep into the thick wall. The other door is L and more slightly made of wood and skins. Both doors are much smaller than those of to-day. They are more like holes in the wall and everyone has to stoop to enter.

There are no pictures on the walls (which are roughly plastered) but here and there again the skins of sheep and goats are hanging, the goatskins being mostly black. A home-made ladder is against R wall. To reduce the size and height of the room the back part is a loft, stored with sacks and old agricultural gear.

The only window is at the back and is a tiny thing rather high up. It should not seem to be more than two feet square and it has horn in it instead of glass, though there were even in those days glass-blowers in Bethlehem. The walls of this house are very thick, as is evident from various deep recesses in them which are used as cupboards, or for storage. One of them at back, which comes into prominence in the action, has various foods in it in dishes and jars, some of which are made of copper or brass and the common red clay. This red pottery is to be seen to a limited extent in other recesses, but they are not in use.

The terms R and L always mean throughout the play stage R and L.

(The Curtain rises on a bright summer afternoon, and there are present ELIAB, AMNON, *and* AMINADAB, *three sons of the*

house, aged respectively about nineteen, eighteen, and seventeen. They are pleasantly if rather greedily eating their supper in different parts of the room, though with the pot on the fire as the centre of attention. All are seated on the floor except

ELIAB, *who is lolling against the ladder.* ELIAB *is a soldier, at home on leave from the army of Saul. His soldierly attire, which is of gay skins, gives a martial touch of colour to the scene. He is fair, the others are dark. They are in thin skins of leather and linen drawers, stockings, and sandals, and are labourers such as tanners, millers, or hewers of wood, and their soiled though coloured garments betray their callings. Their sandals are of undressed leather. All the three are tall country striplings and tend to gesticulate and shout when in dispute as if ready to tear each other to pieces, though it passes in a moment. This emotional exuberance is to be shown at moments by all the characters in the play. They are supposed to tingle with vitality and stress far more than in modern plays. Thus their manners are very unlike the genteel domes-*

ticity of our day. In the opening scene, though they are only gossiping, they do it with as much excess of word and gesture as if the house was on fire. All have wooden bowls in their hands and chunks of home-made bread and they drink from the bowls, occasionally dipping their bread therein. The food is the thick soup of many vegetables, still called Minestrone.

The entrance door opens and SHAMMAH, *another son of eighteen, enters, balancing two old water-skins on his shoulders. He is conscious that this is effeminate employment and scowls at them for implying with mimicry that the water-skins may fall. He, however, carries them successfully through door L.*

AMNON *slips round to look into the bowl of* ELIAB.

About a minute should be filled in thus before there is any talk.

AMNON *points accusingly and dramatically at* ELIAB.)

AMNON. In the name of Israel I call all the world to witness that there is a piece of flesh in Eliab's bowl! (*He shouts as if it were the most dreadful charge.*)

(*There is immediately wild commotion in the Israelite manner, except from* ELIAB *who remains provokingly calm.*)

ELIAB (*placidly superior and holding up the meat in his fingers*).   I claim it as my due—as a soldier of the king.   Observe, Amnon !   (*He devours it.*)

AMINADAB (*passionately*).   We husbandmen must suffer so that the soldier be over-fed !

ELIAB (*gnawing*).   Ay, it is the law.

AMNON.   The other piece of flesh for me !   (*He rushes to the pot and is stirring it, probing it for the meat.*)

AMINADAB.   It is mine !

SHAMMAH.   Mine !

AMNON (*pushing him aside violently*).   The hewer of wood and the baker of bread before the tanner !

(*There is about to be a fight for the meat, but all the youths except* AMNON *withdraw from the pot as their*

MOTHER *enters L.   The name of Jesse's wife I cannot discover, for there seems to be no record of it.   She is a little woman of many cares, somewhat of a drudge, for women were not esteemed of value in Israel ; but this one can nevertheless give*

*blows to her progeny as well as take them
from the august Jesse, and is a determined
housewife, harsh, and without any sentimentality.   She is garbed in her ' working
day '—a short gown with her sleeves rolled
up, an apron of linen, and in her hand a
wooden roller, all to suggest that she has
been baking bread.   She stops to see what*
AMNON *is doing.*

*He does not see her, but the others do and
they await his discomfiture with pleasure.
He is stirring the pot with a short wooden
rod which stands in the pot for this purpose.*)

MOTHER (*like a judge pronouncing sentence*).
Amnon !

    (*He leaps, and she looks as if she could
    leap at him.*)

All of you ravening at your food like wolves in
the morning. (*To* AMNON) You have had your
share. (*She takes his bowl from him and signs to
him to leave the pot.   They all know that she must
be obeyed.*)

    AMNON (*with offended dignity*). I desired
merely to lick the stir-pot (*indicating it in his
hand*). It is my workmanship—with my own
knife I fashioned it—and I claim this small

privilege. (*He licks the stick with as much hauteur as is compatible with the incident and sits again.*)

> (*The* MOTHER *sits near fire and partakes of his bowl.*
>
> SHAMMAH *returns with an empty bowl and approaches the pot.*)

MOTHER (*stopping him*). First, Shammah, have you filled the water-skins ?

SHAMMAH.   Ay, and brought them back—to my shame, for all the maidens at the well jeered at me—a man carrying water like a maid. (*He shouts it like one appealing to the Gods.*)

MOTHER.   Have you tended the kine ?

SHAMMAH.   It is done.   Also I again showed the calf where his legs are, and for what purpose.

MOTHER.   Then make thyself heavy.

> (*The* MOTHER *signs to him that he may fill his bowl, and he does so.*)

SHAMMAH (*with another outbreak*).   Even the beasts have to be fed before Shammah approaches the dregs !

ELIAB.   But assuredly, brother.

SHAMMAH (*shouting*).   It is the part of the youngest to fill water-skins.   Why should *I* have to do the tasks of David as well as my own ? I—I—Shammah !

MOTHER (*snapping*).   Cease your clatter! David is keeping the sheep.

AMINADAB (*excitedly*).   Shammah, hearken to the things Eliab has been telling us of life in the camp! He drinks the blood of the grape!

MOTHER (*with spirit*).   Your father also drinks wine.

ELIAB (*contemptuous*).   From a little gourd!

AMNON (*who considers himself the wit of the household*).   While Eliab, the soldier, drinks it like a horse!

ELIAB (*imperturbable*).   Even so! (*He rises and saunters about.*) The old home! The old pot! (*He surveys the recess that contains his father's supper.*) Behold, Father's supper awaiting his return as of yore, kept coyly within our reach; but which of us would dare to touch? Behold, even his cake of figs. Figs! (*suggestively and wistfully*). Mother? (*He is craving to eat of his father's repast.*)

MOTHER.   Touch not! You dared once, Eliab, to venture upon your father's supper.

AMNON.   Did his staff hurt, Eliab?

ELIAB.   You know better than I, Amnon.

AMINADAB.   It is his belt now.

AMNON. Watch him strutting—Eliab the slinger of the king!

ELIAB (*fiercely*). Scoff not, Amnon, at the slingers of Israel. We are now fifteen hundred men, and the sling we know to be the deadliest of all the weapons of war. (*He takes off his sling, which was carried round the waist like a belt, and makes play with it.*)

AMINADAB. As I shall show them when I too am of the army.

AMNON (*displaying his sling*). And I.

ELIAB. You!

AMNON. With this sling can I already bring thine to shame.

ELIAB. Thus says Amnon!

AMNON. Furthermore, some hold that the bow of the Philistines is more deadly than our sling. So it is said.

ELIAB. Never by Saul.

MOTHER (*as loud as they*). No brawling!

(*They subside, but glare at each other.*)

Eliab, even David has now a sling.

ELIAB. It is no weapon for babes.

AMINADAB. He made it himself.

ELIAB. Ah, that kind of sling.

MOTHER. To be fair to the little worthless, he

brings back many a straying goat with his pebbles.

AMNON. Fear not that he will do you injury with it, proud soldier, for the pebble ever falls behind him, though he points as if it were speeding toward the horizon.

> (*They are all sitting again. Throughout this Act there should be much sitting on the floor.*)

ELIAB. Mother, is David as much a craven as ever ?

MOTHER (*shamed*). Alas, I cannot deny it.

> (*They become quieter for a time, and, though they disparage* DAVID, *there is no real ill-will to him. They are really a good-natured family despite their clamour, and we should like, not dislike, them.*)

SHAMMAH. At his age we others could have helped to fence the walls of Bethlehem.

ELIAB. The seven sons of Jesse, as we are called, for none speaks of the eighth. You who began so well with me, Mother, why did you not desist before David ?

MOTHER. I know to my shame that the child is timid and backward. (*Contemptuously*) The best that can be said of him is that the sheep like him.

AMNON. Yes, he plays to them, Eliab, on his

harp, and they gather round him. They take him for one of their lambs !

(*They laugh over this.*)

AMINADAB. Even our ass is of more account than he.

AMNON. Yea, and David knows it. Hearken, Eliab, when David is from home on it and strangers approach, quickly he dismounts and shows the ass where to hide, for he thinks all covet the ass but that he need not hide himself, for none covets him.

SHAMMAH. I have seen him at such times whisper where it is to hide into the ears of the ass, and lo, that ass does as he directs, so kin are the twain, the one to the other.

MOTHER. I know not what to make of the miserable.

ELIAB (*patting her with kindly intent*). Poor soul ! Yet grieve not over-much. Is not the laying fowl well content if out of many eggs she sits on but one that is addled ?

MOTHER. Talk not of him before me.

AMNON (*mockingly*). Let us rather speak about our soldier brother ! Eliab the Great !

AMINADAB. Ay, tell us, O mightiness, have you ever spoken with Saul ?

ELIAB (*scandalised*). I, a foot man, speak to the king ! Are you bereft, Aminadab ?

AMNON. Bereft ! I have heard that word whispered in the streets of Bethlehem about Saul himself. A traveller of Hebron has brought tidings hither from the camp of a strangeness that comes upon Saul.

ELIAB (*ablaze*). Brother, as you live ! Those words !

AMNON (*scared*). I spoke them not.

(*This is so serious that the turmoil subsides.*)

MOTHER. Nevertheless, Saul was once but a shepherd. I remember a time when there was no king in Israel.

SHAMMAH. In the days of the Judges. No king in Israel !

MOTHER. None before Saul—none but the Lord alone and there was no open vision of Him. The people did demand a king whom they could see, and one Samuel, a mighty prophet of the Lord, did seek out Saul in his fields in Benjamin, and grudgingly anoint him. (*She says it solemnly.*)

AMINADAB. Grudgingly ?

MOTHER. So it is said.

(*Voices get low and cautious.*)

AMNON. The man of Hebron also says there
is now murmuring in the camp of a clashing
between these two, Saul and Samuel.

ELIAB. I say, you spoiler of pelts, there is
none in Israel can trouble Saul and live. Would
you learn how to know a king ?

AMNON. Ay, noble immensity, let us hear and
be wise.

ELIAB. When he comes nigh, though a
stranger to you, your knees give way and you
prostrate yourself before him.

AMNON (*irrepressible*). We thank you, good
Eliab. We are now prepared for the coming of
a king.

MOTHER (*sternly*). Impious youth !

> (*The entrance door is thrown open and*
> DAVID *rushes into the room, breathless with*
> *excitement.*
>
> DAVID *has come down to us from the Old*
> *Testament as ' ruddy, and withal of a*
> *beautiful countenance, and goodly to look*
> *to.' Browning, in his poem ' Saul,'*
> *acclaims him as ' God's child, with dew on*
> *thy gracious gold hair.' As we see him, he*
> *is a child beside his tall brothers. He is*
> *bare-legged and should wear little save a*

*sheep-skin crosswise. His mouth opens
and shuts in gasps as he tries vainly to
give utterance.*)

DAVID. Mother !

MOTHER (*not lovingly, but irritated with him*).
David, what has befallen you ?

(*He gulps.*)

DAVID (*in a glorious mouthful*). Mother, I
have killed a lion !

(*It is so unexpected that the sons leap to
weapons. Next moment the ludicrousness
of the statement convulses them and they
are again loud and demonstrative. Their
mockery of* DAVID *that follows should be
fast and without pauses.*)

AMNON. Our David has killed a lion ! (*He
signs to the others to accept the news as grand.*)
Mother, behold the conqueror !

(*They gather round* DAVID *in burlesque
respect.*

DAVID *in his innocence thinks they are
extolling him, and he presents a proud and
beaming face. He does not notice that the*
MOTHER *has sunk down in shame.*)

ELIAB (*grandly declamatory*). Poor lion that
dared to cross the path of David !

B

DAVID (*ravished with delight over his new popularity*). There was a bear also !

SHAMMAH (*as if further astounded*). Mark that ! There was also a bear !

AMINADAB. There *was* a bear, but there is a bear no longer.

ELIAB. Did the bear pursue you, brother ?

(DAVID *shakes his head exultantly*.)

AMNON. Keep us not in anxiety, boy. Tell us quickly that you also killed the bear, so that fear may go out of us.

DAVID. I did kill him !

AMNON. Mother, the bear-killer.

(*They present* DAVID *to her.*

She turns away her head.)

ELIAB. She is in distress, David, lest the lion and the bear mauled you.

DAVID (*hastening to her to relieve her anxiety*). See, Mother, I have not a scratch !

AMNON (*examining him*). Not a scratch ! Or did you wash the blood from off you at the well ?

DAVID (*it is a new idea to him*). I had not thought of that.

(*The* MOTHER *covers her face with her apron*.)

Eliab, shall we be called the eight sons of Jesse now ?

ELIAB. Your tale first.

AMNON. Ay, let us sit at his feet while he tells us with seemly modesty how he became a man.

(*The brothers sit round him while he stands.*)

DAVID (*gloating*). A man! Amnon, when I went to the fields this morn, I was a boy. (*This reflection rather scares him.*)

AMNON (*as if it were a wonderful recollection*). I remember you as a boy, brother. But the mighty deed?

DAVID (*seeing it with terrifying vividness*). I was sitting in my cave under the rock, and lo, the sheep did eat near by.

AMINADAB. He has now a cave, Eliab, which is almost as big as himself.

DAVID (*jealously*). It is more bigger.

AMNON (*encouragingly*). You were sitting in your cave playing on your harp and——?

DAVID (*easily perplexed*). Was I? I thought I was tending one of the lambs.

AMNON (*politely*). Verily! Well?

DAVID. Suddenly I heard a *roar*!

ELIAB. I quake! Was it the lion or the bear?

DAVID (*trembling horribly*). The lion. It was the biggest lion I have ever seen.

AMNON. And the only one.

DAVID (*a stickler for accuracy*). It was the biggest if I had ever seen more.

MOTHER (*who has been wringing her hands, isolated*). Wretched boy!

ELIAB. Fear not, Mother, for at that moment David strode out of his cave and killed the lion and then the bear.

DAVID. Didn't I? But wait till I tell you how I did it!

MOTHER. Cease, you lying child.

DAVID. Lying? (*He reels.*) Is it all a lie?

MOTHER. Now is the house of Jesse brought low. I had put milk aside for you. But you shall have neither milk nor the pot.

DAVID. O Mother! (*He is bewildered.*)

AMNON (*signing to him to come away from her*). How did you kill them, heroic one? (*confidentially*).

DAVID (*crushed, and stung by his mother*). I have forgotten. I knew, but I do now forget. Perhaps I just nearly killed them.

SHAMMAH. It was thus, David: you would have killed them if they had been there to kill.

DAVID (*catching at this straw*). Wouldn't I, Shammah?

ELIAB. I see what happened. It was a bush of the tamarisk you killed.

DAVID (*with a sinking*). Was it only a bush?

AMINADAB. Courage, it was no bush.

DAVID. No, it wasn't.

AMINADAB. It was one of our father's sheep.

DAVID (*aghast*). One of the sheep?

ELIAB. Worse than that—it was your pet lamb.

DAVID (*in agony*). My lamb?

AMNON. It was neither a sheep nor a lamb. It was a lion.

DAVID. Yes!

ELIAB. But you have got the story wrong; you did not kill the lion, David. It was the lion who killed you.

DAVID. Was that it? (*Hoarsely*) Am I dead, Mother?

MOTHER (*rising—sternly*). Shammah, to the fields to see to the sheep.

SHAMMAH. Always Shammah (*looking at* DAVID) while *he* escapes punishment.

MOTHER. He shall not escape this time. Hasten.

(SHAMMAH *goes out at back.*)

Go from my sight, boy. Your father's belt will deal with you when he returns.

DAVID (*imploringly*). Not Father's belt.

(*She signs to him to be off.*)

(*He speaks cajolingly from the L door.*) May I have my milk, Mother, after the belt?

MOTHER. The manger for you.

(DAVID *goes out L.*

The MOTHER *sits again.*)

Seven sons—and then this one! (*She is a little broken now.*)

(*They gather round her, grieving for her.*)

ELIAB (*kindly*). Harden not your heart against him, Mother, he is but a child and cleaves to folly.

MOTHER (*scorning herself*). There was a time when I thought him wonderful.

ELIAB. So you thought of all of us when we were small.

MOTHER. No, only of him.

(SHAMMAH *returns hastily.*)

SHAMMAH. An old man—a stranger—is in the street asking for the house of Jesse. A hairy man girt in ragged apparel, with a wallet on his shoulder.

ELIAB. I know them, those wanderers who now infest the camp. One of the tribe calling themselves diviners or seers.

SHAMMAH. He looks such a one.

AMINADAB. A mendicant!

AMNON. Maybe a worshipper of gods fashioned by man's hands. Yet I fear them. They have evil spirits. 'Tis said they can turn their faces and walk backwards, and other things as dark. A wizard, Eliab.

MOTHER. May all such be rent from their homes.

ELIAB. They have been. There are no wizards now in the land. Saul has driven them all out of Israel. (*Superstitious*) Yet hold the door against him, Shammah.

MOTHER (*firmly*). Bid him enter.

AMINADAB. See him not. There may be mischief in his wallet.

MOTHER. I fear no one.

> (SHAMMAH *ushers in* SAMUEL. *He was probably the greatest of his kind save Moses, and is a striking figure in this scene and can be alarming, though his entrance is quiet and his habiliments of the poorest, mainly a mendicant's long linen cloak of sombre colourless stuff. His feet are bare. In his hand is a long stout staff and on his shoulder a wallet. He is aged and has a*

beard, grey but not white, and not the long
straggling beard usually given to prophets
in familiar pictures. He can be straight and
arresting on occasion ; he is an aristocrat
in the garb of a travelling priest and strikes
a note of superiority to all around him.
His entrance brings drama into the house.
The manners of all become quieter, re-
strained. It is a noticeable effect of
SAMUEL'S *entrance.*)

SAMUEL (*unostentatiously*). Peace be unto this
house.

MOTHER (*not much impressed by him, but*
civil). You seek my husband, Jesse the son
of Obed ?

SAMUEL. Even so.

MOTHER. It is his house, but he is gone to
Urusalem to sell his pelts. (*Thus was Jerusalem*
then pronounced.)

SAMUEL. I will await him.

(*This liberty the brothers resent but they are*
nervous of him. They are all seated on
the floor themselves.)

ELIAB. You intruder !

MOTHER (*sharply*). Eliab ! (*Courteous but*
cautious) You will break bread in the house of

Jesse, for is not this Bethlehem, the house of bread ?

> (*He inclines his head, and she puts bread before him.*)

AMNON (*sarcastically*).   And thou wilt drink of our water if it be not forbidden to a holy man ?

> (SAMUEL *again inclines his head, and he drinks of a cup which* AMNON *in mock deference presents on bended knee.*)

SAMUEL.   A son of thine ?

MOTHER.   They are all sons of mine.

AMNON.   She has seven sons, O prophet.

SAMUEL (*quite politely*).   Thou couldst have spared one of them for a daughter.   This one (*meaning* AMNON, *as he courteously hands back the cup*).

> (AMNON *is discomfited, but there should never be any straining after comic effect.*)

MOTHER.   If it be alms you seek, your handmaid will find a measure of barley.

SAMUEL.   It is not alms.

AMNON.   He speaks in riddles.   Let us look within the wallet.

> (SAMUEL *has put it down and they approach it.*)

SAMUEL (*sternly*).   Touch not the sacred wallet.

AMNON. Why not ?

SAMUEL. I have hacked a king in pieces for less.

(*They shrink back.*)

MOTHER. What manner of man are you ? For what purpose come you to the house of Jesse ?

SAMUEL. My master sent me.

MOTHER. Who is your master ?

SAMUEL. The master of all.

ELIAB (*impressed*). Of all ? Can it be, good man, that you are as I, a servant of the King ?

SAMUEL (*grimly*). I come not here in the service of Saul.

ELIAB. He speaks to the hurt of the King ! Go, blasphemer ! (*He throws open the door and signs for* SAMUEL *to go.*)

SAMUEL. I go not forth until I have discharged my mission. (*He sits and draws his staff across his knees. He is erect and formidable.*)

MOTHER. Your mission ?

SAMUEL. I was sent hither to find one of the brood of Jesse.

MOTHER. There are three others, but they have taken wives and are no longer in Bethlehem.

SAMUEL. Then they concern me not. I was told I should find him in this house.

ELIAB (*hopefully*). And have you found him ? I am the eldest.

SAMUEL. I wait for my master to tell me.

MOTHER. Your master is coming here ?

SAMUEL. He is here.

(*This is unexpected and startling. He rises to his feet and we see him offering up a prayer, though we do not hear the words. At first the sons are scornful. They have mostly been lolling about on the floor so far to show no respect for him ; but they become impressed and gradually, not all together, but one at a time, they rise and stand reverently though bewildered, the* MOTHER *included. We can see that in the prayer he seems to ask questions and to receive answers.*)

ELIAB. Now do you know which of Jesse's brood you seek ?

SAMUEL. Now do I know that it is none of thee. (*To* ELIAB) Fair of countenance and of goodly stature, I had thought for a moment— but He has refused thee, for man looketh on the outward appearance, but He looketh on the heart, and thou art not the man. (*To* AMINADAB *and* SHAMMAH) Also art thou refused—and thou. (*To* AMNON) Nor hath He chosen thee, poor afflicted one.

MOTHER.   Then your mission——

SAMUEL.   I await the sign.

MOTHER.   The sign ?

DAVID (*suddenly peering in from door L*). Mother, can I have my milk now ?

SAMUEL (*intentionally not looking round*).   Who spoke ?

MOTHER.   Truly I have an eighth son, but he is a child and in a great trespass.

SAMUEL.   Let him be brought before me.

ELIAB (*concealing him*).   He is in the fields tending his father's flocks.

SAMUEL (*still as if unaware of* DAVID'S *presence*). I came hither through the fields which they said were Jesse's, and there was none tending the flock.

AMNON (*mimicking* SAMUEL).   Sawest thou, far-seeing one, aught in the fields but sheep and goats ?

SAMUEL (*who is again seated*).   Lo, I saw a strange sight.   I saw a dead lion.

(*This makes a sensation.*)

ELIAB (*unbelieving*).   How now ?

(*The brothers look at each other.*

AMINADAB *runs out, obviously to make sure
for himself, leaving the door open.*)

DAVID (*emerging into full view of* SAMUEL).
Was there a bear also ?

SAMUEL (*still not looking at him*).   Near the
lion there lay a dead bear.

DAVID.   Eliab ! Amnon !

AMNON.   They must have killed one another.

DAVID (*hotly*).   No, they didn't.

(SHAMMAH *runs out.*)

ELIAB.   They were snared or shot.

DAVID.   No !

SAMUEL.   There was no mark of a weapon
upon them.   Their necks were broken.

DAVID (*gloriously*).   David did it !

(ELIAB *and* AMNON *gape at him and run out
after the others, closing the door.*

DAVID *goes up to* SAMUEL, *who is not looking at him, pulls his cloak, and speaks
shyly.*)

I am David.

(SAMUEL *at last turns, puts a hand on him,
and looks long and seriously at him.*)

DAVID.   Do you think you could get my

mother to give me my milk as I am he who killed
the lion and the bear ?

SAMUEL (*authoritatively*). His milk.

> (*She signs reluctantly to* DAVID, *and he runs
> off L gaily to get his milk*.)

Now, wife of Jesse, leave me with thy eighth son.

MOTHER (*perplexed and incredulous*). Is David
the one whom you seek ?

SAMUEL. I know not yet, but I think he may
be that one.

MOTHER. The sign ?

SAMUEL. David will give it to me.

MOTHER. He cannot know.

SAMUEL. Yet will he give it to me if he is
the one.

MOTHER (*impressed*). I know you not. What
does this presage ?

SAMUEL. Woman, would you have your son
great and terrible ?

MOTHER. There is no danger to him ?

SAMUEL. Mother of David, there is much
danger.

MOTHER. Of all my sons, he is the one that
most needs help.

SAMUEL. No longer perhaps from thee. If he
is the one he will be great and terrible, but *you*

will have lost him.   In all his mighty history you
will have no share.   No record will remain ; even
of the *name* of the mother of David.

 (*She shivers.*

 DAVID *comes back with his cup of milk.*
 The MOTHER *looks after him as he passes.*
 She speaks firmly and thrillingly in answer
 to a look from SAMUEL.)

MOTHER.   I would have him great and terrible.

 (SAMUEL *bows and points to the door L.*
 She goes off L without any faltering and
 shuts the door behind her.

 DAVID *holds up the cup victoriously.*
 About to drink, he offers it politely to
 SAMUEL.)

SAMUEL.   Nay, it is all yours.

DAVID (*finely*).   It is yours and mine.

 (SAMUEL, *pleased with him, just touches it*
 with his lips and hands it back with a bow.
 DAVID *bows in acknowledgment of this*
 generosity, and then has a joyous drink
 that is destitute of manners.)

SAMUEL.   It is good ?

DAVID (*with long-drawn-out ecstasy and his eyes
peeping up over the cup*).   Oo-o !

SAMUEL.   And now tell me how came it to you

that you were able to kill a lion and a bear ?   (*He is seated and he pulls* DAVID *nearer to him.*)

DAVID (*pondering, but chiefly occupied with his milk*). I think it was my lamb. I was in my cave trying to take a thorn from her foot. Then I heard—a roar ! (*The memory of it is so vivid that he seems to hear it again, and he quakes.*) May I hold your hand ? (*He does so.*)

SAMUEL (*encouragingly*). You put your head out of the cave ?

DAVID (*surprised*). Did I ? (*Cautiously*) No, I pulled it in. It was my lamb that put out her head. She did go out of the cave to see who was making that noise. She did not know about lions. Perhaps she thought it was something to play with. Thus are lambs. (*With increasing drama*) Then I peeped out and I saw my lamb in the mouth of the lion. At that—at that——

> (SAMUEL *indicates to him to drink for strength to go on, and*
> DAVID *does so.*)

SAMUEL (*very eager and also excited*). Now is the moment.

DAVID. Something did come over me.

SAMUEL (*triumphant*). You were exalted !

DAVID. Was I ? (*Proud of himself, yet fear-*

ful) I leapt from the cave like a stone from the sling—thus ! (*He demonstrates.*) I did give one roar like unto the lion's roar. (*He makes the sound of the roar, but all is terribly serious.*) I seized him by his beard and delivered the lamb out of his mouth ; and when he turned against me I did twist the head of him—this way—and that way—hold my cup and I will show you.

> (SAMUEL *does so.*
>
> DAVID *shows, with eyes bulging from his head.*)

Thus—till he fell dead with a look of wonder on his face. (*He takes back the cup and finishes the drink, and then speaks with more calmness, as of a smaller thing.*) So likewise did I do to the bear.

SAMUEL (*in a tremor*). You were exalted ! (*He raises his hands to heaven and addresses his God for but a moment and in words we do not hear.*)

DAVID. What is exalted ? To what one were you speaking ? (*Putting down his cup.*)

SAMUEL. To Him who killed the lion and the bear for thee.

DAVID (*indignant*). No, He did not. I did it myself. There was no one there.

SAMUEL. To you the glory.

DAVID. Who is He ? (*Stamping his foot.*)

C

SAMUEL. He is my Master. I am nothing.

DAVID. Where is He ?

SAMUEL. He is here.

DAVID. Here ? Up there ?

SAMUEL. He is everywhere—in the seas—on the mountains. He is in that pelt.

(DAVID *is afraid of the pelt.*)

DAVID. I cannot see Him. I cannot hear him.

SAMUEL. It may not be, with the eyes nor with the ears.

DAVID. How then ? (*He has an idea.*) Now shall I see and hear Him ? (*He covers his ears with his hands and shuts his eyes tight.*) No !

SAMUEL. It will be revealed. You are a simple boy ; but you will become the subtlest of the sons of man.

DAVID. What is subtle ? Is it better than simple ?

SAMUEL (*sadly*). Perhaps some day you will be able to tell me.

DAVID. Then shall we be called the eight sons of Jesse ?

SAMUEL (*as one reading it in a vision*). The other seven sons will bow the knee before you.

DAVID (*enraptured*). They will ? (*Incredu-*

lous) No ?   But if I am one of them, then will my cup be full.

SAMUEL.   It will be such a cup as no other man has drained.

DAVID.   How now ?   (*Eager*) Shall I—see Saul ?

SAMUEL (*grimly*).   You shall see Saul. (*The vision very clear to him.*) Lo, he will search for *you* in all the caverns and recesses of Judah.

DAVID (*pleased*).   Will he find me ?

SAMUEL (*putting the vision from him*).   I trust not ! Soon, David, shall your sheep and you be parted, and the well of Bethlehem will know you no more.

DAVID.   Never shall I leave my sheep. I do love the fold. (*Wondering a little at himself*) Sometimes when I am sitting with my harp in the fields and the sheep bells are pleasant—then do I make thoughts.

SAMUEL (*who is seated*).   Stand there, David, and tell me one of the thoughts you have made while you kept the sheep.

DAVID.   Behold. (*He stands in front of* SAMUEL *with his hands behind his back, like one saying a lesson, and speaks very simply.*) The Lord is my shepherd ; I shall not want. He maketh me to lie down in green pastures; He leadeth me beside the still waters.

> (SAMUEL *rises and looks away, moved.*
> *Then he puts a hand on* DAVID'S *head.*)

SAMUEL (*controlling himself and trying to speak lightly*).   You must finish that thought some day, David.

DAVID (*simply*).   Yes.

> (SAMUEL *is experiencing the loveliest thrill*
> *of a craftsman, the sudden meeting with*
> *another in childhood.*)

SAMUEL.   I welcome you among us, brother. I too am one of those who put things down.

> (DAVID *does not understand.*
>
> SAMUEL *produces a horn of oil from his*
> *wallet.*)

DAVID.   What are you doing?

SAMUEL.   That for which He sent me hither.

DAVID.   The Other One?   (*He closes his eyes and ears again, then opens them, disappointed. He shakes his head.*)   No!

SAMUEL.   Thus I did, once on a time, to another shepherd.   Kneel, my son.

DAVID.   I am afraid.

SAMUEL.   Fear not me.   When you rise I shall be your servant.

(The ceremony of anointing DAVID *here follows. It is brief, as is also the silent prayer which follows. The only words actually heard are those in which* SAMUEL *addresses his God. They are 'I am that I am,' and he says them several times. When this is over he speaks.)*

SAMUEL.   Rise, Master.

*(*DAVID *rises, wondering.)*

DAVID.   Was he here?

SAMUEL.   He was here.   *(He is looking very gravely at* DAVID *when*

The MOTHER *opens the door L hesitatingly.)*
Nay, come, the servant's part is done.

(She comes forward, agitated and perplexed.)

MOTHER.   Will you tell me who you are?

SAMUEL.   I am called Samuel.

(She shrinks back.)
Concerning all you may now hear from the son of Jesse, I warn you keep your tongue in check till I come again hither.

MOTHER *(with some firmness)*.   What you bid me, that will I do.

DAVID *(excitedly)*.   Mother——

MOTHER.   Is the boy safe?

SAMUEL. If you be shrewd. If you have a loose tongue there is now not a step between him and me—and death. (*He holds up a hand as blessing her. Then he prostrates himself before the shrinking* DAVID *and, rising, takes his staff and*
     Goes out R.
     DAVID *and his* MOTHER *gaze at each other.*
     DAVID *is goggle-eyed.*)

DAVID. Why did he do that?

MOTHER (*suspecting much, yet bewildered*). What else did he?

DAVID. He wetted my head from his horn.

MOTHER. What said he? Are you to become a holy man?

DAVID (*his mind in a whirl*). I think I am at the beginning of being holy.

MOTHER. Eat and be strong. (*She hastens to the pot. In a new respect for him she dares to bring him meat from his father's store. There is still no sentimentality about her, but she has awed feelings that he is perhaps to be great.*)

DAVID (*astounded*). My father's supper! (*He eats from his hands, joyfully.*) Mother, I think I am to kill more lions.

MOTHER. If it is that you are to be a holy man, you cannot go about killing.

DAVID (*who is sitting, eating*). Yes, I can. That is what they do.

> (*She is gazing at him, waiting for developments.*)

Mother, I think I killed two lions.

MOTHER. O son, son, you said yourself that one of them was a bear.

DAVID (*determinedly*). There were two bears. (*Regretfully*) Of course He helped me—a little. (*Grudgingly*) He did hold the bears till I finished with the lions.

MOTHER. He—Samuel ? So *he* was there !

DAVID. Not that one—the Other One. That one is nothing. The Other One—He is the One.

MOTHER (*shaking him again*). There was no other here.

DAVID. He was here.

MOTHER. I tell you I watched from the manger. No other entered this house.

DAVID. He was also in the manger. He is everywhere. (*Scared*) Mother, He was in that pelt.

> (*She does not know what to make of it. She brings more food.*)

Father's cake of figs ?

(DAVID *hesitates with a piece of cake on the way to his mouth.*)

MOTHER (*firmly*).   Strengthen yourself, my son.

(DAVID *does so.*)

DAVID.   Mother, sometimes I shall be exalted.

MOTHER.   What is that?

DAVID.   I know not, but when I am exalted, contradict me not, or it will go ill with you, woman.

MOTHER.   What manner is this in which to address me?   (*Becoming more practical*) Poor child, your brothers will soon buffet this vaunting out of you.

DAVID (*cheerfully*).   I shall admonish them, and then they will bow the knee before me.

(*She is proud of him again.   She brings the dates.*)

Father's dates!

MOTHER.   Jesse!   I heard him alight from the ass.

(DAVID *wipes the remnants from his face. He is apprehensive.*

She pushes him down.)

Do you remain there, still as salt.   He must hear naught save what I see fit to tell him, and that will only be about the lion.

DAVID. Mother, I think I am now to be exalted.

MOTHER (*wringing her hands*). Not before your father.

> (JESSE *now opens the door R, and the* ASS *follows with various loads on it. The door L had been left open, when the* MOTHER *came out, and this* ASS, *well knowing its home, goes straight through by itself.* JESSE *shuts the other door and comes in. He is a rough-bearded man of about fifty, of medium height, of the strong, small farmer type, in skins and leggings and a sheep coat. He mutters a 'Peace to the house' and stretches himself and stamps. He knows* DAVID *is there by the fire, but* DAVID *is too insignificant to take special notice of. The* MOTHER, *a solicitous wife, helps him off with leggings and other things as they talk. His appearance suggests one who loves sheep, eats sheep, and dreams sheep, and could almost speak sheep.*)

MOTHER. Was the road heavy, Jesse ? You are late.

JESSE (*with the good-nature of one who has had a good day's business*). There is no road for the time being—this most blessed rain—and I was delayed by the haggling in Urusalem—but the pelts bartered well. (*He sits.*) Give me to drink.

(*She ascends ladder on R, to the loft.*) Has anyone sought me?

MOTHER. Only an old man—one of those wanderers in rags.

JESSE (*with distaste*). Ugh!

MOTHER. But I told him you were in Urusalem, and he soon passed on his way.

JESSE. So is it always in this little place. Nothing ever happens in Bethlehem.

(*She has brought down the wine-gourd and he drinks from it with satisfaction.*

DAVID *has been sitting staring, inconspicuous, and she wants to get him out of the way.*)

MOTHER. See to the ass, David.

JESSE. He tend the ass! Since when has Jesse returned from a journey and let any but himself do that? Ay, even before I break bread. (*Going L.*) But I am as hungered as one lost on Mount Nebo. Do you bring me my supper, and I will eat as I provender the ass.

MOTHER (*realising that she can defer no longer —afraid*).   O Jesse!

JESSE.   What now?   (*He sees something is untoward, and comes back.*)

> (*She shrinks.*)

MOTHER.   Your supper, Jesse!

JESSE.   Is not all as I enjoined?

MOTHER.   I prepared it for you.   But I thought : Jesse lingers, he is supping at the rest house ; and I ate it—see the empty shelf.

JESSE.   You ate my supper!   (*He advances upon her threateningly.*)

> (*She shrinks.*
>
> *The frenzy of exaltation is now upon* DAVID *and he rises.*)

DAVID.   Reprove her not, for I say it was I who did eat thy supper, down to the cake of figs and the dates, and lo, they were good.

JESSE.   Is this David?   (*He takes off his belt ominously.*)   And you encourage him!   (*He again advances on the* MOTHER.)

DAVID (*protecting her*).   Lay not thy hands upon her—I command thee, Jesse son of Obed, put down that belt.

> (JESSE *lowers the belt in bewilderment.*
>
> *The* MOTHER *is astounded.*)

MOTHER.   Even Jesse obeys him !

JESSE (*furious*).   *I* obey him ?   (*He suddenly shrinks back in religious fear.*)   Is he possessed ?

MOTHER.   He has killed a lion.

JESSE (*shrinking back from him*).   Possessed ! And is it so also with you ?

MOTHER (*entreating*).   I will tell you of him. Come.

> (JESSE, *keeping his distance from* DAVID, *goes out L.*
>
> *The* MOTHER *is following ; she turns back for a moment.*
>
> DAVID *is quivering from head to foot.*)

MOTHER (*she would fain help him*).   Son of Jesse !

DAVID (*who is now about the middle of the room, isolated, while she is near the door L*).   I know not who or what I am. Something frightens me.

MOTHER.   Samuel—he who was here—he may not have passed beyond the walls. Shall I seek him and bring him back to you ?

DAVID.   He cannot help me. Not that one.

> (*In despair she goes off L, without closing the door.*
>
> *After a moment's woe,* DAVID *looks at the*

pelt, then upwards as SAMUEL *had done.*
He has inspiration. He closes his eyes and
ears and calls.)

Other One, David is in darkness. Will you
not tell me what to do ? (*Appealing*)—Other
One ?

(*When he opens his eyes and takes down his*
hands, a great change has come over him.
He is radiant, all excitement has passed
from him. He is normal and serene, an
ordinary happy boy. Evidently he has got
his answer. He produces his sling, which
has been round his waist, unobserved so far.
It is such a sling as boys of to-day often have
—made at home. He sits on the floor,
testing the sling and cleaning out his pouch
which was, according to the Old Testament,
a shepherd's bag or scrip.
The MOTHER *looks out at doorway.*
He hears her. He nods to her three times,
meaning that all is lovely. He speaks
happily and briskly, but like an ordinary
boy making a casual statement.)

DAVID. Mother, I am to go to the camp
of Saul to slay another lion. I am to go on
my father's ass. I am to take my sling (*he*

holds up sling and picks up his harp) and my harp.

> (*This little programme is far from relieving
> her. She is more perplexed than ever.
> She goes out L, closing the door behind her.*
> DAVID *is alone, boyishly engrossed in his
> sling.*)

CURTAIN

ACT II

ACT II

SCENE 1

SAUL AWAITS

This is a Front Scene from which there is to be a change occupying the whole stage.

It is an open-air scene, twelve miles distant from Bethlehem, near the camps of Israel and the Philistines. These camps, however, are not visible, though their proximity is suggested by occasional martial sounds from a distance, of trumpets, horns, etc. We are supposed to see a height on the edge of a wood, which wood is continued on the back cloth into mountainous country and should be recognisable as characteristic of Palestine in those days. That is, the trees should be in height little more than what we would call bushes. Palms, oleanders, vines, olives, figs, sycamores were the native trees (except at distant Lebanon, famed for its cedars), and an occasional mighty Terebinth (or turpentine) tree. The Israelites are supposed to be massed unseen beyond the wood on stage L and the Philistines on R. (The time is the morning

D

of the following day, early in autumn.) **A**
trodden path in front from L to R, and here a
slight clearing of trees. The only 'practical'
properties are a bundle of little tree trunks **R**
and a sloped bank **L.** *Against the bundle of*
trunks is a formidable-looking javelin, belonging
to Saul.

> *(The only person on the scene is* JONATHAN,
> *son of Saul. He is a boy of about* DAVID'S
> *size and age of twelve, and must be played*
> *by a real boy. He is cultured, good-looking,*
> *and intelligent, but not imaginative, and*
> *his chief note is of open honesty. He is*
> *attired in armour, mostly of leather, which*
> *is ornamental rather than useful, for he is*
> *considered too precious to be risked. He is*
> *looking* **R** *dejectedly, and an occasional*
> *horn or trumpet is heard from back, not*
> *suggesting activity but merely camp routine.*
> *These sounds he disregards. He comes and*
> *sits on the tree trunks, distressed.*
> *To him there hurriedly enters from* **L** *a real*
> *fighting man,* OPHIR, *a young captain of*
> *Israel.* OPHIR *is brave and devoted to Saul,*
> *though presently we see that he can be rather*

complacent and thick-headed. He salutes
JONATHAN.)

JONATHAN (*remaining seated and glad to welcome a friend*). You, Ophir ! You seek my father ?

OPHIR (*in an excited state*). Ay, Prince Jonathan, I seek the King. I was told I should find him here—far from the camp. My King, far from his camp ! (*It is a cry of anguish, with the Israelite excess of voice and gesture.*)

JONATHAN (*dispirited*). You find Jonathan alone, Ophir, and Jonathan is downcast.

OPHIR (*treating him as a boy and going to him kindly*). I grieve, my lord Jonathan, that you are downcast. (*In a blaze*) But of the downcast is every captain, ay, and every foot man in the army of Israel these forty days.

JONATHAN. None more than Saul himself. Look on him, Ophir.

(OPHIR *looks R.*)

OPHIR (*with passionate devotion*). My King !

JONATHAN. See how irresolutely he paces— backwards and forwards.

OPHIR (*in horror of the idea*). Saul grown irresolute !

JONATHAN. Ophir, I think a distress has

come upon him. I have seen him with his eyes open, yet he saw me not, and I have touched him and still he knew me not and muttered to himself.

OPHIR (*he speaks low and guardedly*). I have heard of a night when the cry went forth, ' Behold a dark spirit troubleth the King.' And servants were sent out to seek a cunning player on a harp and he played before Saul, and the burden was lifted off him.

JONATHAN. Think of it. He gazes north, south, east, and west, for a prophet who never comes.

OPHIR (*grinding his teeth*). This Samuel !

> (*A distant horn and trumpets answering produce an outburst from him.*)

Why falls he not upon the Philistines now drawn up against him ? A King heretofore sweeping his enemies before him, and to-day more like one with clothes rent and with earth upon his face ! (*Begging*) My prince, come to our aid !

JONATHAN. Ah, my friend, he looks upon me as a child, decked in the trappings of war, but shielded from the fray (*scorning himself*). That is all we are, my pretty armour and I.

OPHIR. Know you that he even forbids us to take up the challenges to single combat thrown

across our lines by insolent Philistines ?   There
is among them one Goliath who tries us sore,
strutting before our outposts daily and crying
that Israel cannot find a champion to stand up
against him.

JONATHAN (*boyishly*).   Goliath ! I have heard
of the monster Goliath.   Ophir, you must take
me to see the sight.   Is it true that he is beyond
mortal bulk, in a harness of unbeaten brass, and
that the staff of his spear is of the thickness of
a weaver's beam ?

OPHIR.   Truly, the story grows with the telling.

JONATHAN.   Ophir, if we are in such a strait,
why do the Philistines wait for *us* to strike ?

OPHIR.   It is a cunning enemy which knows
that our army weakens as the bread becomes
spent in our vessels.

JONATHAN.   See, my father's javelin.   As he
moved away he left it here, as a thing of war
and therefore of no account.

OPHIR.   The javelin of Saul ! (*He treats it
with reverence, then kisses it.*)

JONATHAN.   Why did you kiss it ?

OPHIR.   In forgiveness, my lord Jonathan ;
for when I have said my say to Saul I have a
sinking that this javelin will enter into me.

JONATHAN (*reproving*). You speak thus of the sweetest master !

OPHIR (*fervently*). He is, he is ! But who has countered Saul and lived ?

JONATHAN (*looking R*). He comes back—haste away, Ophir. Leave your words to him unspoken.

OPHIR (*firmly*). What I have to say I must say. (*As one saying good-bye to life*) Israel, farewell.

> (SAUL *comes on from R. He should be presented in the play as a noble figure in Israel's history, though the clouds have begun to gather and he is to be a broken column. He is dark-bearded and at most about forty years of age. For an idea of his appearance a study should be made of Rembrandt's famous picture of David playing before Saul, which, however, is a conception of much later date, and all the garments in the play must be of those Israelite days.*)

SAUL. You bring word from Samuel ? (*He is quiet and dignified.*)

OPHIR (*who has saluted him*). There is none, O King.

SAUL (*concealing his feelings*).   Then trouble me not further, good Ophir.

OPHIR (*on his knee*).   My King, I pray you, hear me.   Your captains drew lots who should hazard this, and it fell upon me.   Forty days have we lain here, ready but not striking. There is murmuring in the tents ; deserters steal away by night, and the ranks of the Philistines swell as ours diminish.   (*Aware of his daring*) Your captains, O King, beg—they demand— that the battle be engaged.

SAUL.   Demand !   (*He becomes dangerous, but retains his kingly quality*) Take heed to yourself, Ophir.   You know the temper of my blood. Now is your head in jeopardy.

OPHIR (*bravely*).   As one about to be slain, O King, I speak the words given to me to say. 'The battle now,' they cry, or 'Does a priest rule in Israel ? '   (*He bows his head as offering it for the stroke.*)

> (SAUL *is very threatening and half draws his sword.   For a moment there is silence, and then he controls his passion.*
> OPHIR *looks up with a brave smile.*)

Am I still alive, O my King ?

SAUL (*with the charm that sits so well on*

monarchs). Shake your head, Ophir, and let me
see. Ay, it seems not to fall off.

OPHIR. For a moment I thought it to be
severed.

SAUL. For a moment perhaps it was. You
faithful servant, I return it to you. (*He graci-
ously helps* OPHIR *to rise. He moves away and sits
on the tree trunks. There is a smile on his face.*)
Now shall we converse more intimately of Saul
and his transgressions ? (*He points to the ground.*)
    (OPHIR *sits on it near him.*

    JONATHAN *is on the sloped bank.*)
(SAUL *is still gentle.*) Ophir, who would reign if
he could lay down his kingship ? Not Saul, not
for another day. (*It is an honestly meant statement, but it is not in accord with Jonathan's
knowledge of him.*)

JONATHAN. *You* say that, Father !

SAUL (*smiling like one found out*). You will
know it, Jonathan, when you are king after me.
(*Fervently*) To be nameless for ever and my tomb
unknown—the boon of boons ! What else say
my captains ?

OPHIR. They say that a priest's place is not
where two armies stand drawn up, the one
against the other.

SAUL. Never more, my friend, than then. The charge may not sound till the Blessing comes from on high—(*lowering*) and Samuel brings it not.

JONATHAN. Must it come through Samuel? Have you not told me, Father, that the Lord speaks to you direct?

SAUL (*sternly obedient to his God*). Thus has it been in the past. But now He seeks me out no more, as if His face is turned from me, and He repents that He has made me great. Only through Samuel will He answer me—and Samuel comes not. I must await His bidding, for it is the Lord and not Saul who is King over Israel.

OPHIR (*uncomfortably*). To your captains it looks as if this prophet ruled. Are the days of the Judges come back? Your captains would know whether you more love Samuel or fear him.

SAUL. I love him as my own soul.

JONATHAN. Oh, Father!

SAUL. (*defending himself*). There was a time when I loved him even thus, and so has Samuel seemed to love me. (*His fingers suddenly twitch to be at the throat of the prophet.*) Yet now if I could—— (*He controls himself.*) But he is a holy man, and we must all bow before holy men—even kings. I am vowed to this waiting till he comes and I get his bidding to fall to.

> (*The venom of it makes them draw back.*
> *They hear some sound from off L.*
> SAUL *signs to* OPHIR, *who draws his sword and goes L. He returns.*)

OPHIR.   A messenger from Samuel!

> (SAUL *indicates that he is to be brought forward, and from this moment the King is a subtle one, holding himself in check and concealing his real feelings though his mind is seething.*
> *A guard, rough-bearded and wearing a loin skin of leather, brings in the* MESSENGER *who is a young priest with the fire of asceticism on his face. The* MESSENGER *makes ungracious obeisance.*)

SAUL.   Your message, Nathan ? Comes the prophet hither ?

MESSENGER.   Samuel says thus unto King Saul—' I will not come to thee nor will I look again upon thee.'

OPHIR (*outraged*).   Will not ! (*He advances upon the* MESSENGER.)   This fellow——

SAUL.   Nay, he seems a friendly soul and finds favour in my eyes.

(*The puzzled* OPHIR, *who is of plodding mind, though he is not aware of it, signs to* GUARD, *who goes off L.*)

Was it not Samuel who, in a day far past, sought me out in my fields in Benjamin, but I had gone thence to search for my father's asses ?

MESSENGER.   Thus I have heard did Samuel.

SAUL.   When he found me did he not anoint me King ?

(MESSENGER *makes a grudging assent.*)

Who sent him to Benjamin for that end ?   And why ?

(MESSENGER *is reluctant to reply, but* SAUL, *quite quiet, forces it out of him.*)

Come, answer me.

MESSENGER (*reluctant*).   It was the Lord— Who even then was loth to have anyone over Israel save Himself alone.

SAUL.   Yet was I sought out in the smallest of the tribes in Israel, I who was content in my fields, and thus had my life disturbed.

MESSENGER.   It was done because of this stubborn people, who clamoured for a visible king.

SAUL (*stoutly*).   Ay, a visible king—such as other nations have.

MESSENGER (*imperiously*).   There are no other nations.

SAUL (*humbly*).   It is so.   For are not the pillars of the earth the Lord's, and hath He not set the world upon them ?

MESSENGER.   Now you say truly.

SAUL.   Nevertheless I ask how He who is omnipotent did *need* to bow to the wishes of a clamorous people ?   (SAUL *is perhaps being more subtle now than the* MESSENGER *had expected of him.*)

MESSENGER.   Need !   Have you never asked yourself why you, of little Benjamin, were chosen ?

SAUL (*confidently*).   It was because I had the most kingly qualities.

MESSENGER (*for once smiling at him*).   Ay, you have loved being a King !

SAUL (*with simple dignity*).   I have loved it.

MESSENGER.   And never saw that such a one as you were chosen as a punishment to Israel for its clamour !

SAUL (*to whom this is a shock, but controlling himself*).   Punishment ?   Was that just to Saul ?

OPHIR (*in rage*).   Let me speak——

SAUL (*stopping him with a gesture*).   I asked and I have been answered.

MESSENGER. For long the Lord succoured you, seeing you as one little in your own eyes.

SAUL. Since then have I not, as He enjoined me, ever gone into the battle in front of my people—striking always the first blow ?

MESSENGER. Not your people—His people.

SAUL. Ay, His, yet all who had known me in Benjamin marvelled at the wisdom of my words, crying, ' What is this that has come over the son of Kish ? '

MESSENGER. And what was it that had come over you ?

SAUL (*sadly*). I vowed to strip this base tenement of its littleness. To serve the Lord without ceasing till I join those who dwell in dust. Such, when I became King, was the vow of Saul too recent from the plough to know his own wild heart. I had ever meant to go the way I was sent.

MESSENGER. When you were ordered to destroy the Amalekites, men, women and sucklings, every one and their sheep and their oxen, did you go, Saul, the way you were sent ?

SAUL. I spared the sheep and the oxen—it was as spoil for my soldiers, for only thus are battles won.

MESSENGER (*scornful*).   Only thus—in Israel ?

SAUL (*humbly*).   I spoke hastily.

MESSENGER.   You also sought to spare one of the Amalekites—the man Agag.

SAUL.   Because he too was a King.

MESSENGER (*contemptuously*).   You Kings !

SAUL.   In that again I sinned.

MESSENGER.   And showed your repentance by building at Carmel a trophy to the glory of the conqueror Saul ! With a crown upon your head. Who said that Saul might wear a crown ?

SAUL.   If I had hearkened not to my Master, I sought to atone by making sacrifices—(*losing his humility*) with a sufficiency of blood even for Him !

MESSENGER.   To obey is better than sacrifices and to hearken better than the fat of rams.   You would be the one-over-all. He who was once little in his own eyes has become too much a King. Thou seest thyself lifted up to the skies like a cedar of Lebanon—*and the Lord wearies of you.*

SAUL (*stung*).   Is it that he is jealous of Saul ?

MESSENGER.   Now dost thou reveal thyself !

SAUL (*scared*).   I meant it not of Him but of Samuel.

MESSENGER.   For long Samuel interceded for you, and seeking to placate the wrath, he did himself hew Agag to pieces before your eyes. But at last Samuel removes you from his presence.   Take now from me the words I bear from him, and *heed them well*.

JONATHAN.   This to my father !

SAUL (*again controlling himself and as one obedient to messengers*).   Say on.

MESSENGER.   Thus says Samuel unto Saul : ' Get your battle in array, for this day shall the Philistines fall before Israel.'

OPHIR (*exultant*).   This day !

SAUL (*with a smile, though undeceived*).   You like the prophet better now, Ophir !

OPHIR.   I had misjudged him.

SAUL.   Be not too sure of that.   I think our gentle messenger has more to say.

MESSENGER.   I have more.   This day, says Samuel, shall the first blow be struck—but not by thee, O King.

OPHIR.   What is this ?

SAUL.   Let our soft-spoken one proceed.

MESSENGER.   When the sun is hot there will come through the tents of Israel one riding on an ass.   To him shall be the first blow.

SAUL (*with polite interest*). While the King to whom hitherto has always been the first blow——

MESSENGER. While the King stands aside and waits : *for thus it is decreed.*

OPHIR. This messenger craves for the sublimity of death.

SAUL. Ophir, you are hasty. (*To the* MESSENGER) And if I hearken not to the commands of your master ?

MESSENGER. Then woe unto Saul, for a boy will rule in thy place.

SAUL. Are you in such hurry, Jonathan ?

MESSENGER. Thus ends the message of Samuel, whose prophecies ever come to pass. (*He makes a defiant bow.*)

SAUL (*still in his baffling mood, which is beginning to puzzle even the* MESSENGER). What say you, Ophir, how shall we discharge this messenger ?

JONATHAN. Grant him his craving, Father, and let him be quit of life.

SAUL. Thus to a messenger ? (*As if in great good-humour*) Nay, Ophir, fill our friend with honey and the grape and speed him courteously upon his way.

MESSENGER. I am of the holy seed, and I will not eat nor drink of thine.

SAUL (*becoming grim*). If he refuses my bounty, thrust it down the gullet of him till he expands. Saul swears in this, his hour, to be kingly unto all. (*An explosion of cold fury follows.*) Carry this to your prophet, O priest: Greetings from Saul to Samuel the man of the suspicious eye. Say he has made a King of me again. Inasmuch as he dared not obey my summons hither but sent his croakings by thee from some place of hiding, now I know he fears my wrath when I thought 'twas I feared him— and lo, is his hand lifted off me. I am delivered.

MESSENGER. This is forbidden.

SAUL. Forbidden! Tell him from me that what is forbidden, that shall I do. I dismiss him from my service. Let him not again call himself prophet, or I will put him to the saw and the lime-kiln.

MESSENGER. The Lord——

SAUL. Him shall I serve as ever when I hear His voice—(*defiantly*) but I will not serve Him through the voice of Samuel. He must speak to this King direct.

MESSENGER. Now art thou doomed.

E

SAUL (*sternly*).   Go.

> (OPHIR *is exultant though startled.*
>
> JONATHAN *has been drinking it in, open-mouthed.*
>
> *At a sign from* OPHIR *the* GUARD *returns L.* SAUL'S *eyes are fixed on the* MESSENGER, *who makes a cowed but not cowardly exit with the* GUARD *L.*)

OPHIR (*glorious*).   Now is Israel redeemed ! (*He kisses* SAUL'S *garment.*)

JONATHAN. You said well, Ophir. There is none can counter my father and live.

SAUL (*well satisfied with himself*). A boy will rule in my place ! Ay, is it so ? Jonathan, are you in such undutiful haste to reign ?

JONATHAN (*embracing him*). Looks it so, thou poor prophet ?

> (*Horn heard.*)

OPHIR. 'Tis as if Israel already rejoiced with us.

SAUL.   Ay, it shall be battle now—and Saul's the first blow ! Thus shall Samuel learn that I—I . . . (*A terrible thought comes to* SAUL *and stops his utterance.*)

OPHIR. This day is Samuel overthrown. (*Coming towards* SAUL, *he is startled by the change in his face.*)

JONATHAN. King! King, my father. Ophir, see his face!

> (SAUL *signs with his hand to* OPHIR *to come to him. When* OPHIR *approaches,* SAUL *speaks to him as one puzzled in a blank voice.*)

SAUL. Who are you?

> (*This should be the first intimation that something has happened to him.*
>
> *It comes also as a sudden shock to* OPHIR *and* JONATHAN, *who look at each other. It should all be very quiet.*)

JONATHAN (*in apprehension*). Father!

SAUL (*to* OPHIR *coaxingly*). Come tell me who you are.

OPHIR (*shuddering*). I am Ophir, one of your captains.

SAUL (*politely, but evidently not understanding*). Captains? (*With some cunning*) And I? Truly I know who I am—but how am I called?

OPHIR. You are Saul the King.

SAUL (*blankly*). King? Tell me, soldier, what is this anguish that has come upon me? Did I hear a voice? (*He means the voice of the Lord.*)

OPHIR (*as in the presence of the supernatural*). None spoke.

JONATHAN.   Oh, Father !

SAUL.   And this one ?   Who is he ?

OPHIR.   This is Prince Jonathan, your son.

SAUL.   Son ?

JONATHAN.   My father !

>   (*As* SAUL *looks at his son, recognition comes to him, and he speaks lovingly.*)

SAUL.   Jonathan ! (*The darkness passes from him slowly and he is the King again. He clasps the boy to him.*) Some voice disturbed the balance of my mind. (*He remembers.*) My son, this Samuel, how do I know what he meant——? (*his face becomes dreadful with malignancy—he speaks sternly*) Ophir, as you would live, say to none that you have seen me thus.

OPHIR (*steadily*).   I have seen nothing.

>   (SAUL, *brooding, goes to sloped bank and sits.*)

SAUL.   Leave me.

>   (OPHIR *goes off* L *with a reluctant look at* JONATHAN.
>
>   JONATHAN *nervously kneels on bank to the* R *of* SAUL *but close to him.*)

JONATHAN.   Do not send me from you.   Is it that something in the prophet's words disturbs you ?

SAUL (*who is staring L and not looking at him*). It concerns you not. (*Grimly*) Ay, it concerns you! But go (*royally*)—the King would be alone.

(JONATHAN, *disturbed, goes off L behind the bank.*)

(*Now in sombre thought with* SAMUEL'S *words in possession of him*) ' A boy will rule in my place.' How do I know that Samuel means Jonathan? (*He is sitting staring L, immersed in this thought and held by a fixed idea.*)

(DAVID *now enters R, riding on his ass, and his small harp is slung on his back. He is not ' exalted ' at present, he is the cheery shepherd boy, and he and his ass are on the best of terms. He pulls up R when he sees the figure on the bank.*)

DAVID. Greeting, friend.

(SAUL *does not hear.*

DAVID *dismounts and hesitatingly approaches the stranger, but prevents the ass following him. Evidently, as told in the first Act, he fears that here is another one who might covet the ass. He whispers lovingly into its ears unheard words. He points R to some place where the ass is to*

> *keep out of sight. It signifies understand-*
> *ing with its ears and makes an exit R, and*
> *he signs to it to go further and lie down.*
> *When he is satisfied he addresses the stranger*
> *again.*)

Greeting, friend. Is it that you can say how I
may get me to the camp of Saul?

SAUL. Did I not tell you to go! Yet wait.
(*He rises, and in his present state though he sees*
DAVID *plainly he presumes it is still* JONATHAN.
He leaps as it were at DAVID, *and putting a hand*
on his shoulder walks the astonished boy backward
and forward, pouring out his emotion in a torrent.)
Jonathan, know you of any in high places with
sons who may be aiming at the throne? You
know them better than I. Ahiab, son of Alihab
—he will be great in Judah—what of him? Or
Shetnel—he has a snarling lip for one so young.
It might be Ishbaal the Philistine, out of my
own household.

> (DAVID *breaks away from him.*)

DAVID. What is this? I am David, the son
of Jesse.

> (SAUL *is now the bewildered one. He*
> *looks around for* JONATHAN *and ' comes*
> *to.'*)

SAUL (*roughly*).   You seem to be a country boy.   Who are you ?   What do you here ?

DAVID (*rather frightened*).   I am David, son of Jesse.

SAUL.   I know no Jesse.

DAVID.   I did but halt to ask you how I may get me to the camp of Saul.   My father is of Bethlehem, and there I do tend his sheep in the fields.

SAUL.   Sheep ?   Ay, truly, I see them in your eyes.

DAVID (*disturbed*).   Do you ?

SAUL (*who sees that he is being taken literally*). And I hear the sheep-bells in your voice.

DAVID (*fearing that there must be something wrong with himself*).   Can it be so ?

SAUL.   Sheep !   I too, boy, have led the sheep home, as many times as there are stones upon the road to Jericho.   I was a shepherd—once— myself.

DAVID.   Were you ?   You do not look so now. What is your name ?

SAUL (*introducing them, with a touch of humour*). Son of Jesse, I am—the son of Kish.

        (DAVID *bows.*)

DAVID.   Was your land fat or lean ?

SAUL. Here and there were fat parcels of ground—but the barren places, David! (*He begins to be amused by* DAVID.)

DAVID (*sympathetically*). I know! How I know! *And* the goats in the barren places— waiting to pounce if one blade springs up. How many sheep had you?

SAUL. Five hundred, it may be, when I returned from a fray.

DAVID (*astounded*). Five hundred! No! And kine?

SAUL. I forget how many.

DAVID (*scandalised*). *Forget* how many!

SAUL (*seating himself and speaking with apparent gravity*). Listen and direct your ways. I had two camels and an olive press, and my well was bricked.

DAVID (*gasping*). Bricked! (*Boasting*) Nevertheless there is no water like to the well of Bethlehem which is by the gate.

SAUL. That may be so, but I had a fig-tree that bore twice in the year.

DAVID (*who stands near him with legs wide apart and head thrust forward—impressed*). Truly you were in a big way! We have a hundred sheep and twenty goats, he's and she's. (*Making the*

best of his case) My mother has a flagon shaped
like a camel and two painted glasses.

SAUL (*handsomely*).　I never had that.　But,
David, I had——

> (SAUL *is falling under the spell of* DAVID,
> *who takes it all seriously.*)

DAVID.　Do not tell me you had a he-goat
that danced.

SAUL.　Ah me, none of my goats danced.

DAVID (*proudly*).　Two of my father's goats
dance, as thus.　(*He shows.*)

SAUL.　Would that I had seen them !　But,
David, I had three fields of onions.

DAVID (*overthrown*).　Three—fields—of onions !
(*Anxiously*) But had you a vine that grew upside
down ?

SAUL.　Never.

DAVID (*ashamed of boasting*).　Neither had we.
But my father travelleth far.　Consider of this.
He has seen—a bed with four legs !

SAUL.　What a man is this Jesse !　Now shall
I learn, David, whether thou art worthy of such
a father.　Behold, a shepherd sits bowed over
his staff in woe, the sheep lie on their backs,
the kine give no milk, and your two he-goats
can dance no more.　Then the shepherd smells

—what does he smell, David, that causes him
to dance with the he-goats and the she-goats
and makes the grass to arise and dance with
them ?

(DAVID *has been listening anxiously*.)

DAVID (*with a shout and making several syllables
of the word*).   Rain !

SAUL.   A stream ran through my land, David.

DAVID (*incredulous*).   With water in it ?

(SAUL *nods*.)

No !

SAUL.   Now tell me (*unbelieving*)—if you can
—what is the tree in which there is ever a
whispering as of voices in the highest branches ?

DAVID (*after reflecting*).   The mulberry !   There
is always a going-on in the tops of the mulberries.
(*He is getting wildly excited*.)

SAUL.   This one will defeat you.   At what
time of the year had I and my servants—men
and women—at what season of the year had we
all purple legs ?

DAVID (*gloriously*).   At the treading of the
grape !   (*He jumps up and down to show how it
is done.   Then, in an outburst, he cries :*) Shall we
be friends, O Shepherd ?

SAUL (*like a boy*).   We are.

DAVID.   You do look a fine one in that cloak.

SAUL (*amused*).   Do I, David ?

DAVID (*who has been leading up to this*).   How do you think I look in mine ?

SAUL.   Lo, it is good. (*He puts a hand on* DAVID'S *shoulder and walks him back and forward.*)

DAVID.   My mother made my coat.

SAUL.   *My* mother, I do remember, used to make mine !

DAVID (*finding this a remarkable coincidence*). Did she ?   We are very like each other, Shepherd.

SAUL.   The likeness between us grows every moment !   Did your mother also make your harp ?

> (*They occasionally stop for a moment in their walk and talk and resume walking.* DAVID *is sometimes walking backwards in front of* SAUL.)

DAVID.   Oh no.   My father did want to belt me for having a harp, but my mother dissuaded him.

SAUL.   A good, but perhaps weak mother.

DAVID.   She is not weak !   She will let none belt me but herself.   (*Standing up for her*) There is in all Bethlehem no woman who can lay on as my mother does.

SAUL. On you ?

DAVID. Verily. (*Gloomily*) It is my appetite.
Sometimes she does slip food into my mouth
before it is due ; and then she is angered, for
behold when I have eaten heartily there is
nothing about my person to show for it. Then
does she at a time lay on.

SAUL (*laughing*). Son of Jesse, I have a drawing to you.

DAVID (*who is often getting in front of him to
look up in his face happily*). Have you, Shepherd?

SAUL (*jestingly reproving*). But this appetite
of yours——

DAVID (*recklessly*). I do also drink ! Hearken !
Coming hither I did see some kine in a field, and
I milked one—but my mother has told me never
to take without paying, so I did tie half of my
bag of provender on to the tail of the cow.

SAUL (*delighted*). Now is this like an hour of
my youth in Benjamin come back to me !
David, you should first have bound her hind
legs together lest she was with calf, and treacher-
ous. I always did that.

DAVID (*victoriously*). She *was* with calf. And
so I did bind her hind legs, even as you did !
Assuredly we are as one.

SAUL. Even so.

(SAUL *so evidently enjoys this that* DAVID *is prompted to say, after a manner of his own :*)

DAVID. Now you tell *me* why you like *me*, and then will I tell *you* why I like *you*.

SAUL. Let me see. I believe you are close to me because I was such as you when a boy. (*Adopting his manner*) Now do you tell me why you like me.

DAVID. I think it must be because I want to be such as you when I am a man.

SAUL (*laughing*). Oh, artful one ! But I had forgotten. Tell me, what brings you to seek your way to the camp of Saul ?

DAVID (*regretfully*).   Now do I become subtle.

SAUL (*smiling*).   Oho !

DAVID.   Do you now ask why I become subtle, and lo, I will tell you.

SAUL.   Why have you become subtle, son of Jesse ?

DAVID.   I have become subtle because my mother did say : ' Tell naught of why you have set forth to any who may question you on the way, lest they make merry and despoil you of your belongings.'

SAUL (*amusedly*).   I am rebuked. (*He sits again.*)   David, we are two subtle ones, you and I !

DAVID (*gleeful*).   Are you also subtle ?

SAUL.   Ay, but it is not subtle of you to come hither.   All these paths lead to the camp of Saul, and the neighbourhood of camps is ever dangerous.

(DAVID *nervously goes and sits close to him.*) Why do you do that ?

DAVID.   Because if there is danger to me, I feel safe if I am near you, Shepherd.

SAUL (*grimly*).   All have not found safety so close to me, David.   But take this token with you and show it to any guard who would bar your way. (*He gives him the token, which is a metal disc about two inches long and one broad.*) It will clear all paths for you.

DAVID.   How do you know ?   Does Saul say this ?

SAUL.   Saul says this.

DAVID.   Have you ever seen Saul ?

SAUL.   I have seen him.

DAVID (*old-fashioned*).   How is it with him ? Is he in good health ?   Sleeps he well ?   Are kings like men ?

SAUL. I sometimes think, David, that Saul is like two men.

DAVID. Are there two of him because he is a king?

SAUL. Ay, so it must be with kings. There are two within Saul—the one good—the other a roaring lion.

DAVID (*pricking his ears at the word*). A lion! Why does not the good one in him slay the lion?

SAUL. I wonder! Perhaps Saul rather likes his lion!

DAVID. Does he? Do all the people love Saul?

SAUL. Nay! He has his enemies, David, and there is talk of a new unknown one. You have made me forget him. Now we must part. (*He pats the head of* DAVID *and rises*.) Fare you well, son of Jesse, and fortune attend you.

DAVID. So also may it be with you, son of Kish. And may that enemy of Saul be rooted up and cast among the slime!

SAUL (*grimly*). As my soul liveth, he shall be!
    (DAVID *goes off R, waving a hand. His
    voice is heard off-stage :*)

Shepherd Man!

SAUL. Thou Child of Dew!
    (*He communes fiercely with himself.*)

Was it Ahiab Samuel meant—or Shetnel or Ishbaal? ' A boy will rule in thy place.' It must be one of those three. (*He rises.*) Not this time, Samuel, shall your prophecy come to pass. Saul shall wax greater and greater. (*His hand closes on the javelin.*) There is naught like being a King, and King I will abide.

(*He goes off L, muttering :* ' Ahiab, Ishbaal, or Shetnel.')

End of Scene 1

SCENE 2

DAVID AND GOLIATH

The scene is an out-post of the slingers in advance of the Israelite army. They occupy rocks on stage L. The rocks on stage R are presently to be occupied by Philistines, but are at present empty. They should be more sloped and grassy. Between the opponents is a glade which covers the centre of the stage. This glade is still pointed out in Palestine to the credulous as the scene of the fight with Goliath, so that it can be reproduced to some

*extent on the stage. It was called the Vale of Elah,
which means 'oak' (so there were probably oaks
there in those days).*

*The time is the same day about noon, and the
sun is hot.*

*At back the outlook is partly cut off by rock,
but there is an opening C and on the back-cloth
toward L is a suggestion of Saul's innumerable
tents—which were mostly of black goat-skin. They
are some distance away and are mere dots in the
landscape. We should realise that there is a small
plain behind the rocks at back. All the rocks are
'practical.' It is a scene where characters can come
and go variously, i.e. from the opening at back, up
and down the rocks, or down stage on both sides.
There should be, wherever it is most convenient
scenically, a trickle of water falling into a pool.*

*(The Curtain rises on a scene of wild
tumult between* ISRAELITES *and* PHILIS-
TINES, *though the latter are unseen and are
shouting from off-stage R, the idea to be
suggested being that they are about twenty
yards away. No command to attack having
as yet been given by either side, those clashes
at out-posts are no more than brawls. A*

F

number of the ISRAELITES *rush into the glade and up the rock R but do not go out of sight.*

The attire of the PHILISTINES *was at once more gay and showy than that of Israel. They varied, as there was no fixed uniform, but shining breastplates, brass helmets, feathered head-dresses were common, and they had better arms and were better disciplined. Their horse-chariots were dreaded by the* ISRAELITES, *who were practically all foot men. At present there are not at the moment more than twenty men visible. They are* SLINGERS *of Israel. The* SLINGERS *carry their slings, but the ban against fighting is still in force and the* SLINGERS *are prohibited from using their weapons. They, however, demonstrate with them as they shout. It is mainly an outburst of cries and vituperations of a deafening kind between the seen* ISRAELITES *and the unseen* PHILISTINES, *so that the actual words are little heard though they will be supplied. They are animals thirsting to be at each other in an eruption of barbaric declamation and big gestures such as are incon-*

*ceivable nowadays : shouts, taunts, etc.,
poured forth across the glade like lava,
and the wildness of the scene can only be
rendered by a producer acquainted with the
stage representation of Old Testament turbu-
lent incidents. This turmoil should last,
at most, not more than two minutes and be
like a bonfire—a leap of flame, then suddenly be burnt out. It ends with the blow-
ing of a horn from the unseen Philistine
ranks. An immediate silence follows, and
the effect is to make all the* ISRAELITES
*drop into hiding, so that they seem to have
disappeared.*

The PHILISTINES *appear noisily escorting
an important person. They settle on their
rocks as he proudly descends into the glade.
He is the* ARMOUR-BEARER *of Goliath,
finely and picturesquely attired, and with
a bugle round his neck. He is a young man
and, though self-important, must not be in the
least farcical, for nothing may be done to
mar the drama of the scene. He stands in
the glade and sounds a defiant note on his
bugle. Then he addresses the concealed*
ISRAELITES.)

ARMOUR-BEARER. Wake up, you Slingers of this out-post of Saul, and listen to me, the Armour-bearer of Goliath. Find you not that forty days sufficeth you for one sleeping? Come out from the rocks where you are hiding, and hearken again to the challenge of my master, Goliath of Gath.

ALL. Come out! cowards.

ARMOUR-BEARER. Nay, then, lurk in your hiding holes, you dogs, till he sends servants with whips to lash you out.

FIRST PHILISTINE. We are the whips!

SECOND PHILISTINE. The whips of Goliath!

ARMOUR-BEARER. Thus says Goliath: ' Am I not a Philistine and ye the cravens of Saul! Go out into your camp and search among all your captains, and let one come there to the Vale of Elah where Goliath awaits him.'

ALL. Your champion.

ARMOUR-BEARER. ' Then shall the tent of Goliath become his and the spear of Goliath become his. But if I prevail against him and kill him, then shall ye be our servants and serve us, ye and your Gods.'

ALL. You shall be our servants.

THIRD PHILISTINE.   The servants of the men of Goliath !

(OPHIR *jumps up fiercely but* JONATHAN *pulls him out of sight.*)

ARMOUR-BEARER.   There is no man among you, no, not one ! Dogs of Israel, the challenge is still open. Get you a champion. Haul him hither by a rope. His bugle has but to sound, and Goliath is ready. (*He again blows his challenge.*)   Behold !

FOURTH PHILISTINE.   Get you a champion.

ALL.   Haul him !

ARMOUR-BEARER.   His bugle of defiance has but to sound, and lo, the spear of Goliath will be ready in the vale.

(*He returns up the rocks R, blows his bugle, and they all exit exultantly.*

There is now no one left on the Philistine rocks.

The Captain of the Slingers, ABNER, *signals to the* ISRAELITES *to arise, and they do so, raging at the indignity they have had to endure. Some of them leap into the arena, slings in evidence, to pursue the* PHILISTINES, *but he drives them back.*)

A SLINGER.   You dogs.

ABNER. We may not fight. The King forbids.

A SLINGER. Skulkers ! It is what we are !

ANOTHER. Ay, it is what we are.

ANOTHER. If we may not let loose our slings, why should we carry them ?

ANOTHER. If we may not fight, why carry our slings ?

ANOTHER. To show no longer are we fighting men ?

A THIRD. Down with our slings, I say—no longer are we fighting men.

ALL. Down with our slings !

(*Several throw down their weapons.*

ABNER *draws his sword on them.*)

ABNER. Up with your swords or you shall die by your Captain's hands.

A SLINGER. We have no Captain who could stand up against him.

ALL. We have no Captain.

ANOTHER. Must we wait another forty days till *our* horn answers ?

OTHERS. The horns of Israel are broken.

ALL. Broken, broken, the horns of Israel are broken.

(*An unseen horn, different in tone, is heard*

*from back at R as from some distance, low
yet clear, and all are stirred.*)

A SLINGER.   Did you hear ?

ANOTHER.   Some one accepts the challenge !

ANOTHER.   Who could he be ?

ABNER.   If only I could be he !

ANOTHER.   A champion for Israel.

ALL.   A champion for Israel.

OTHERS.   At last !

ANOTHER.   He comes down the hill.

A SLINGER.   Where is he ?

ANOTHER.   Now he is behind a rock.

A SLINGER.   Where ?

ANOTHER.   Over there.

ANOTHER.   Now I see him.

ANOTHER.   He comes this way.

(*Similar cries from* OTHERS.)

ALL.   He comes !   He comes !

A SLINGER.   He comes.

ANOTHER.   A boy.   Lo, it is a boy riding on
an ass !

(OTHERS *crowd round up-stage and their
excitement changes into mirth.*)

Behold the champion of Israel !

(DAVID *comes riding forward at back on the
ass and with a horn in his hand.   He is in*

*his exalted condition, and it should have
the effect of keeping the scene serious, which
is essential. He is now a boy of high re-
solve, with no playfulness about him.*)

DAVID (*with dignity*). Greetings to this out-
post of the Slingers of Israel. (*All murmur
'Greetings.'*)

ABNER (*roughly*). Whence come you ?

DAVID. I am David, the son of Jesse, and
lo——

ABNER. I care not whose son you be, nor do
I believe you ever had parentage. What seek
you here ?

(OPHIR *and* JONATHAN *enter.*)

DAVID. I say unto you, speak not thus of
my parentage, and I seek here a lion who is
called Goliath of Gath.

ABNER. And when you have found him ?

DAVID (*calm and resolved and simple, and without any boasting*). Then shall I slay him.

ABNER. With your sling or with your harp ?

DAVID (*with dignity*). It is to be with my
sling.

A SLINGER. Behold the champion of Israel !

DAVID. Deride me not because I am a boy.
This day shall I slay Goliath.

A SLINGER.   What say you ?

ANOTHER.   Hast ever heard the like ?

ANOTHER.   This poor Goliath !

(*His quiet assurance impresses the* SLINGERS,
and they are perplexed and ponder.)

A SLINGER.   What cast of boy is this ?   (*All
start murmuring*.)

ABNER (*also puzzled*).   What I would know is,
how came it to pass that they let you ride un-
checked through the camp of Saul ?

DAVID.   All were kind and sped me on my
way, and they did give me this horn on which
to blow my challenge, and behold I will blow it
again.   (*He is about to do so*.)

ABNER.   Hold him !

SEVERAL.   Hold him !

(SLINGERS *restrain* DAVID.)

A SLINGER.   They sped him on his way !

ANOTHER.   It is unbelievable——

ANOTHER.   Yet the poor soul believes it.

ANOTHER (*with awe*).   Is he bereft ?

DAVID.   I am not bereft.   I am exalted.

A SLINGER.   There are things happening in
these days that pass the wit of man.

(OPHIR *and* JONATHAN *have remained down
L in this scene, hardly noticed ; but they*

have listened intently, and OPHIR *now comes forward.*)

OPHIR. Abner !

ABNER (*relieved to see a superior officer*). Now are you pleasant in my eyes, Ophir, for you are a captain of five hundred and I but of fifty, and there is that to decide which I shall gladly leave to you. This boy——

OPHIR. I have heard all. (*He signs to the* SLINGERS *to stand back.*)

(*They do so, but keeping hand on the ass on which* DAVID *still sits.*)

ABNER. What to do with him ? There is something untoward about this boy.

OPHIR. Ay, more so than you know of. I have known it since he came here riding on an ass.

ABNER. He says that all he met in the camp encouraged him on his way.

OPHIR. Ay, but that I *cannot* believe. (*He goes to* DAVID.) Say you, boy, that no guards opposed your coming hither through the camp to this uttermost out-post of the slingers ? How could it be so ?

DAVID. At first they did stay me ribaldly, dragging me from the ass and otherwise mis-

using me, but when I showed it to them they
all did speed me on my way.

ABNER.   They were mocking you.

OPHIR.   What showed you to them that did
make so great a man of you ?

DAVID.   This which he gave me. (*He puts the
token into the hands of* OPHIR, *whom it startles.*)

　　　(*He shows it to* ABNER.)

ABNER (*equally taken aback*).   The token of
Saul !

OPHIR.   Ay ! (*He calls to* DAVID.) How came
you by this ?

DAVID.   A shepherd did give it to me in a
clearing in the wood.

ABNER.   Shepherd ?

OPHIR.   He was once that. (*To* DAVID) How
did he look ?

DAVID.   He did look noble, and he sat on an
open space in the wood in a purple cloak, and
a javelin was near by.

　　　(OPHIR *and* ABNER *exchange glances.*)

OPHIR.   He spoke with you ?

DAVID.   He did so. He is my greatest friend,
and I am *his* greatest friend.

OPHIR (*to* ABNER).   Be wary, Abner, the boy
knows not who it was. A shepherd he be-

lieves; and so Saul wants him to believe. What do you conceive is now in the secret mind of Saul?

ABNER. The token of the King! No thinking is needed. All know its meaning: 'Do as the Bearer asks, or incur the wrath of Saul.'

OPHIR. Ay, so it means—and what asks this Bearer?—To fight Goliath!

ABNER. That turns it all to folly.

OPHIR (*grimly*). Does it? Let me think. (*He moves about, brooding.*)

(ABNER *goes to* DAVID.)

ABNER. Now would I make amends. If you will be pleased to alight——

DAVID (*with dignity*). It is my pleasure. (*He alights and examines his ass solicitously.*) It is a valuable ass (*rubbing his head on it*). Also I do love it.

ABNER. It shall be in my charge, well tended.

DAVID. Peace be yours, O ass. I shall come to see how it is with you when I have slain this Goliath.

(ABNER *gasps at this, but evidently gives orders to a* SLINGER *who mounts the ass and is going with him up-stage.*
DAVID *frowns.*)

DAVID.   Who is he that doth mount my ass ?

ABNER.   His name is Hiram—your ass is safe with him.

> (*The ass turns its head and looks oddly at* ABNER.)

DAVID.   The ass may be safe with Hiram, but Hiram is not safe with the ass.

> (HIRAM *rides the ass off L at back.*
>
> *Immediately they are out of sight a scuffle is heard off.*
>
> DAVID *cannot see what has happened, but he explains to* ABNER.)

DAVID.   Hiram is no longer on the ass.

> (*The* SLINGERS *hasten to see what has happened.*
>
> DAVID *and* ABNER *go with them.*
>
> *For a brief space* OPHIR *and* JONATHAN *are alone on the stage.*
>
> OPHIR *in his broodings meets* JONATHAN *down-stage, and has shown him the token.*)

JONATHAN.   Let the boy go unharmed, Ophir. You can see what hand has touched him—he is afflicted.

OPHIR.   My prince, do you forget the words of but an hour ago—' One who shall come riding on an ass ' ?

JONATHAN.   Samuel did not say a boy.

OPHIR.   He said : ' To that one who comes riding on an ass must be given the first blow, or a boy shall rule in the place of Saul.'

JONATHAN.   He meant me.

OPHIR.   So we thought, but it has now come to me that this is the boy he meant—and so I believe has it come to the King. (*This is a shock to* JONATHAN.)   What asks the boy ?   To fight Goliath.   What orders this token ?   To grant him that boon !

JONATHAN.   Of death !

OPHIR.   Ay, but in that one stroke he is removed for ever from the path of Saul.

JONATHAN.   Poor shepherd boy !

OPHIR (*whose loyalty to his King is still a redeeming feature*).   See you not also that, with the fate of the boy, Samuel falls in the eyes of Israel ?

JONATHAN.   The people know not that this champion is the choice of Samuel.

OPHIR.   Mine the part to let them know.

JONATHAN.   If thus my father wanted he would have made his meaning clear.

OPHIR.   Kings speak not their wishes clear but leave it to their servants to interpret them.

JONATHAN.   Consider your peril, Ophir—what if you interpret him awry ?

OPHIR.   I have considered it.   Yet even if I err the King would still be unharmed.   He would but seem to have followed in the way he was told.   This prophet is a deep one, but he shall find that I am deeper.

JONATHAN.   It is not, I think, the deepness of you that commends you to the King.   If you read him wrongly now——

OPHIR (*finely*).   It would be the end of Ophir, but what matter if I was seeking to serve Saul ?

JONATHAN (*touched by his devotion*).   Truly you love him !

OPHIR (*passionately*).   Ay, do I !
      (*Shouts and declamation of the soldiers
      as they return.   ABNER pushes forward
      in front of them.*)

A SLINGER.   Away with the child.   Thus say we all.

ALL.   All.   All.   All.

OPHIR.   How now ?

ABNER (*who has DAVID'S horn in his hand*). His horn.   They took it from him, crying that to let such a one face the man of Gath would be to make sport of us before the Philistines.

(*Cries of corroboration of this rend the air*—
' We will not have him—Shall Israel be
shamed ?   What means Saul by giving us
such a champion ? ')

OPHIR.   First hear me.

(*The turmoil subsides.*)

Israelites, the boy comes not from Saul, he is
the choice of Samuel.   Saul scorns this champion,
but Samuel proclaims that this boy and no other
shall strike the first blow.   For forty days has
Saul hungered to fall upon the Philistines, but
he cannot because he has been under the weight
of a vow to the Prophet.

FIRST SLINGER.   A vow to the Prophet ?

SECOND SLINGER.   Saul is under a vow to
Samuel.

THIRD SLINGER.   I have heard of this.

FOURTH SLINGER.   What is this vow ?

FIFTH SLINGER.   We know this vow.

SIXTH SLINGER.   It is not to fight.

SEVENTH SLINGER.   Samuel orders it.

EIGHTH SLINGER.   Yes, he orders it.

NINTH SLINGER.   Does Samuel rule in Israel ?

TENTH SLINGER.   Ophir, speak.   Tell us why
Saul obeys him—this Samuel.

OPHIR.   I bring word to you from Saul.   Thus

says Saul to his people, 'Let Samuel have his wish.' At such a moment what is the life of a boy or the triumph of a braggart ? Samuel's be the shame.

ALL. Yes, Samuel's be the shame.

OPHIR. For listen, soldiers. With that first blow Saul is absolved of his vow ! Then will he straightway give battle.

ALL. The battle ! The battle !

FIRST SLINGER. Saul will be absolved of his vow !

SECOND SLINGER. The forty days are over !

ALL. The forty days are over !

OPHIR. See him again this day, Israel, as you have been wont to see him in your front, Saul our King, as he bends backward, astride your enemies, his javelin in his hand. He calls to you once more to smite the Philistines.

ALL. Smite the Philistines !

OPHIR. Then shall their cattle be thine, and their wines and their horses and their camels shall be thine, and their chariots shall be thine, and at last there will be workers of iron in this land to forge us swords and spears. Are you ready to be magnified, O Israel ? Is it to be the battle ?

(*His outburst is gradually received with clamorous cries of* 'The battle, the battle —the forty days are over. Let the boy perish — Hail the King,' *ending with* 'But where is the boy?'

DAVID, *who has been neglected and lost to sight, is now discovered in a parting of the crowd, quite regardless of them, testing pebbles in the water.*

They regard him wonderingly.)

ABNER.　What are you doing, boy?

DAVID (*loooking up*).　I am gathering pebbles for my sling.

A SLINGER.　Truly this one is not as others are.

DAVID (*to* JONATHAN).　Who are you, boy?

JONATHAN.　My name is Jonathan.

DAVID.　My name is David.

DAVID (*more secretively*).　Hearken, Jonathan. They say that he who kills Goliath acquires his tent and his spear.

JONATHAN.　It is so, but woe unto you.

DAVID (*very worried*).　I fear not to sleep in his tent if there is a lamp. But his spear! Jonathan, if his spear is like unto a weaver's beam, as they say, how shall I be able to carry it on my shoulder?

JONATHAN (*astounded*).   Is that all that in this dire moment afflicts your mind ?

DAVID.   It is chiefly that.

JONATHAN.   Thou pitiful !

A SLINGER.   Ophir, are we men that we can give him to the spear of the Philistines ?

OPHIR.   It is not we who give him.   It is Samuel.

A SLINGER.   Ay, true, it is not Saul who sends this one to the man of Gath.   Samuel's the blame.

ALL.   Ay, Samuel's the blame.

OPHIR.   The boy's own be the decision.

A SLINGER.   Death awaits him.

ANOTHER.   Let the boy do as he will.

(OPHIR *takes horn from* ABNER.)

OPHIR (*who sees that he must act quickly before a fickle crowd*).   This is his horn.   Let him sound it if he dares.

(*He casts the horn on to the glade where* DAVID *is alone.*)

ABNER.   Know, boy, there is none in Israel who will face this monster.

A SLINGER.   None.

ALL.   None of us.

ABNER.   For he is as one left over from the

giants who were drowned in a deluge and now mourn and groan in Hell beneath the waters. Such is this Goliath, crying mockingly that Israel is without a God.

DAVID.   Who is the God of Israel ?

ABNER.   Our Maker, the Lord of Hosts, Whom this Goliath defies.

DAVID.   Can it be ?   (*He looks up, shuts his eyes, then crosses to where the horn lies.*)

JONATHAN (*coming to* DAVID).   Touch not the horn, David.

A SLINGER.   Touch not the horn.

JONATHAN.   Surely now, you are afraid.

> (DAVID *shivers, and for the moment his courage is gone.*)

OPHIR (*jeering*).   Ah, see how Samuel's champion trembles !   In vain do we await the blast that was to be great in the history of Israel.

A SLINGER.   He fears !

DAVID (*though still in a quiver and rather child-like*).   Perhaps I am afraid—but thus does David.

> (*He lifts the horn and blows a clear challenging blast.*
>
> *The answer comes from the Philistine*

camp. *All cringe and work around to the L of stage.*)

ARMOUR-BEARER (*off-stage*).   Goliath awaits the champion of Israel.   Here in the Vale of Elah.

ALL.   He is doomed.

(*The scene becomes darker.*)

A SLINGER.   A darkness comes upon the land.

ALL.   A darkness comes upon the land.

A SLINGER.   Who sends it ?

ANOTHER.   The Lord deserts us.

ABNER.   Or has the boy a friend we know not of ?

OPHIR.   He has no friend.

(*The stage is now quite dark.*)

ARMOUR-BEARER (*off*).   Goliath awaits.

(*Challenging trumpets are heard from Philistine camp. All the Israelites creep away, leaving only DAVID and JONATHAN.*

DAVID hesitates, then slowly walks up centre and goes toward the Philistine camp. He backs, appalled by what he has seen. JONATHAN creeps up to him.)

JONATHAN (*in whisper*).   David ! David, did you see him ?

DAVID. I saw him.

JONATHAN. What think you ?

DAVID. He is of a size even more huge than they said. Jonathan, I am not *quite* sure now that I shall win.

JONATHAN. Fly with me quickly, David. I can save you still.

DAVID. No.

GOLIATH (*off*). Now shall Israel be shamed for mocking me with such a champion. Look, insect, upon Goliath of Gath.

DAVID. Lo, I have looked and you are smaller than they said.

GOLIATH. How many pebbles, little one, are in your wallet ?

DAVID. There are five, but I think I shall not need them all.

GOLIATH. I curse thee by my Gods. Come to me and I will give thy flesh to the fowls of the air and to the beasts of the field, thou Israelite who art without a God.

DAVID. Thou comest to me with a sword and with a spear and with a shield, but I come to thee in the Name of Him Whom thou hast defied. This day will He deliver thee into mine hands and I will smite thee,

that all the earth will know there is a God
in Israel.

(*Poised on the rock,* DAVID *discharges his
sling at the unseen* GOLIATH. *The stone
whistles through the air. There is a moment
of intense silence, followed by the echoing
sound of* GOLIATH'S *fall.* DAVID *runs off-
stage in the direction from which the sound
comes. The darkness gradually lifts, and
one by one, very slowly and anxiously,
Israelites come on, bewildered and unable
to understand what has happened. They
do not speak, but stare in the direction of
the Philistines.* ABNER *is amongst them.
This situation lasts a full minute. Suddenly an Israelite comes on from the side
of the Philistines, crying breathlessly and
hoarsely:* ' David has slain Goliath !
David has slain Goliath ! David has slain
Goliath ! ' *Repeating the same words again
and again like a madman, hc crosses the
stage until he disappears from sight.
Behind the scene you still hear him repeating this incredible news—spreading the
miracle through the tents, his voice growing
louder. The few men on the stage are*

awestruck, whisperingly asking one another,
' David has slain Goliath,' *as though unable to believe their own words.*

Then there comes a long-drawn cry from the Philistines, ' David has slain Goliath ! ! ! '
With barbaric dancing and wild shouts Israelites pour on to the scene until the stage is quite full. Throughout all the clamour the words ' David has slain Goliath ! ' *are continuously heard, taken up by more and more of the thronging Israelites until at last the sentence rises to a jubilant roar.*

Finally DAVID *comes on with* GOLIATH'S *great spear. Being unable to raise it, he is dragging it along the ground with both hands.*

The Israelites dance wildly around him until one cries out : ' The battle ! The battle ! ' *This idea is taken up by more and more, until with one accord they all rush off in the direction of the Philistines, their voices mingling in one unanimous cry :* ' The battle ! The battle ! ')

End of Scene 2

SCENE 3

DAVID PLAYS BEFORE SAUL

*It is the night of the same day, and it is the same
Scene, except that the tent of Goliath now occupies
a conspicuous place in it; and as much of the action
is to occur inside this tent, all other matters must be
subservient to a complete view of not all but most
of the inside of the tent to everybody in the house.
This will require much stage-craft and practical
consideration.*

*The tents of those days were not white, they were
indeed mostly black, made of the skins of black
goats, etc., but we can suppose that Goliath's tent
was of a barbaric and bizarre appearance, such as
had appealed to his crude imagination, and it is of
skins of various animals sewn together. It has a
centre pole and, when open, the inside should
follow, as far as may be, the picture already re-
ferred to by Rembrandt of David playing before
Saul. It must be down-stage, not in centre, but
nearer to L than to R, and the opening, which is
sometimes closed, must be to the footlights. It must
be of considerable size, and will cut off the view of a
large part of the scene, but this does not matter.*

*A general effect will be got, in glimpses, of the
former scene, with the army tents now lit up here
and there and moving lights, and where there is
talk or important business outside the tent, it is to
take place down-stage R where the tent will not
obscure the actors. The lighting of the scene can
vary for stage effect, but on the whole it is a dark
night, and no moon is visible.*

     *(The effect to be got when the Curtain rises
is as if it had risen prematurely on stage-
hands putting the finishing touches to the
erection of the tent, but the workmen are
Philistine prisoners, and overseer to them
is* ABNER, *who is doing it with a whip,
which, after the manner of the times, he does
not hesitate to use. There is quite a suggestion of savage cruelty. Some of them are in
chains, all are sullen and crouching figures
and one of them is Goliath's* ARMOUR-
BEARER.
     This opening of the scene is to convey its
meaning without words, and is to include
the carrying to the tent of Goliath's helmet
and armour and rich rugs. When* ABNER
thinks it is finished he relinquishes his

whip to an Israelite GUARD, *who drives the captives away in front of him amid the jeers of the conquerors.*

The tent has been closed so far, and a light shows through interstices in the covering.

DAVID *and* JONATHAN *are inside but unseen, and the tent is already lit up before rise of Curtain.*

Simultaneously there is revelling going on upon the rocks on both sides as well as suggested in the distance. There is music and singing in barbaric joy and leaping over an Israelite victory. The whole thing is of the briefest, as all the appearances of crowds in this play are, but it is furiously wild while it lasts. It is ended abruptly about the same time as the departure of the captives by loud blasts from off-stage, which signify the recall of the revellers to camp. They go quickly but still revelling.

ABNER *is now alone and troubled. He surveys the tent.*

OPHIR *comes from back, rather furtively, and they meet down-stage R.*)

ABNER.   Ophir !

OPHIR.   Ay, he has let me live but I am no

more a captain. Heard you not the recall to camp sounded, Abner ? (*As one dismissing him*) We are no longer needed here.

ABNER (*looking at tent*). Yet would I linger —ay, till the morning light.

OPHIR. Is the boy within his tent ?

ABNER (*ill at ease*). Yea, and Prince Jonathan with him. Ophir, why has the tent of Goliath that is now David's been pitched in this lonely place ?

OPHIR. Guards have been left him on the rocks. Does he complain ?

ABNER. Nay, he is too ignorant to know fear so long as there is a light within. So was it with me, in the days when I was small. (*Touched*) The two of them are playing with the harness of Goliath. He is now more like a child than a conqueror.

OPHIR (*grimly*). Then all is well.

ABNER. I do not think that in this dark glade all is well. (*Looking round the dark glade*) I think there is danger this night to David.

OPHIR (*lowering*). Who can be the enemy ? Say to me his name, Abner !

(*Obviously* ABNER *could say it but he shrinks, afraid. He listens suspiciously.*)
For what do you listen ?

ABNER.   I seem to hear the beating of a heart that is privy to wickedness.

OPHIR.   Come, come, thou troubled one, have not the Philistines been consumed ; and their camels, ay, and their horses and even their chariots are now the servants of Israel.   All shout this night to the glory of the King whose name you are afraid to speak.

ABNER.   Ay, truly, they exult in the King. But they also cry (*he looks significantly at the tent*) ' There is no boy like this boy ! ' and because of thee, Ophir, they whisper, ' Great is Samuel who sent to us this champion.'

OPHIR (*shuddering*).   Speak not of it !   Does David know now who his shepherd is ?

ABNER.   I asked Prince Jonathan to say naught of that to him.

(*Bugles are heard again.*)

OPHIR.   The second horn.   Come, Abner, I shall go with you.   All make revel to-night save I !

ABNER (*shivering*).   Not all.   I was here alone when the first of the darkness came.   I was *not* alone.   There was evil flitting through this glade.

OPHIR (*similarly moved*).   Then let us avoid out of its presence, come.   As my soul liveth, never again shall I say of him, whose name we both fear to speak, that he needs aid save from his own javelin.

> (*They go off with a last furtive look at the tent. As far as possible their exit should be visible from all parts of the house.*
>
> SAUL *comes on and picks up his javelin which is leaning against the tent.*
>
> *A sound from the tent arrests his attention. It is* JONATHAN, *speaking as he emerges. He comes through the slit without opening it and calls in.*
>
> SAUL *has moved up-stage.*)

JONATHAN.   Truly, David, this time I must go. It was the second horn. (*He comes out.*)

> (SAUL, *coming back, meets him R down-stage.*)

You, Father ! (*He is afraid of him.*)

SAUL (*lowering*).   Again with this boy ! (*Pouring it out*) You son of the perverse rebellious woman, do not I know that you have chosen this son of Jesse to your own confusion ? Jonathan, for as long as this David liveth upon the ground, you shall not be established in this kingdom.

JONATHAN.   If so it be, he knows nothing of it.

SAUL.   That shall I now learn. (*In another rush*) My son, it is you shall follow after me

over Israel—ay, though the Lord Himself say
no! (*Clutching his javelin—secretly*) Jonathan,
get you to your tent; it is not Saul you have
seen here to-night; know *that* when you wake.

JONATHAN (*alarmed*). Father, send me not
from you!

> (DAVID *puts his head through the slit in the
> tent.*)

DAVID. Jonathan, did you call? (*He comes
out and is bewildered.*)

JONATHAN. It is the King!

> (SAUL *frowns but has to dissemble.*)

DAVID (*enraptured*). No, it is not, Jonathan—
it is my Shepherd. (*He bends with his hands on
his knees, boy-like, and gazes gloriously at* SAUL.)
Son of Kish!

SAUL (*now a crafty man*). Son of Jesse, we
meet again.

DAVID. Let me encompass thee. (*He clasps
SAUL round the legs. In glee he calls out:*) Shepherd,
know that I am the one who slew Goliath!

SAUL. I have known it for an hour. Hail to
the conqueror!

DAVID. Jonathan, it was he gave me the
token! (*To* SAUL) Lo, all the greatness of David
has come to me from you.

SAUL (*grimly*).   Ay, verily, so I have learned.

JONATHAN.   Father——

DAVID.   Why do you call him that ?

JONATHAN.   He is Saul, the King !

> (DAVID *gapes and looks at* SAUL *for corroboration*.)

SAUL.   Even so.

DAVID.   Now if you will swear it to me by my sling, then will I do something.

> (SAUL *is for the moment captured by this*.)

SAUL.   By your sling, I am the King.

DAVID.   Stand away, Jonathan, I know how to do it.   (*He makes space for himself, and then prostrates quite prettily before* SAUL.)

> (*The third bugle sounds and* SAUL *points imperiously to* JONATHAN.
>
> *Exit* JONATHAN *with misgivings*.)

(DAVID *rises and speaks shyly*) Was that right, O King ?

SAUL.   It was well done.

DAVID.   Has Jonathan gone ?

SAUL.   Ay, it was the third horn.   Shall we go into your tent, David, and talk—but on a different matter ?

DAVID (*gaily*).   Let us.   (*He stops* SAUL.)   Nay, first wait till I clap my hands.   Next, do you

pull the opening both ways—wide—and then—
lo, you shall see what you shall see.

(SAUL *nods.*

DAVID *disappears into the tent.*

SAUL *makes sure to his satisfaction that he
is alone in the glade—he ponders darkly.
The clapping of the hands is heard. He
pulls the opening of the tent to its widest and
then looks at the picture that has been
prepared for him.*

It is DAVID *standing majestically, posing
as* GOLIATH, *with the helmet on his head and
his two hands grasping the hilt of the spear,
which is otherwise trailing on the ground.*)

DAVID (*motionless*). What think you ?

SAUL (*who finds it difficult not to be enamoured
of this boy*). Is this the man of Gath come back
to life ?

DAVID (*pleased, but reassuring*). Not truly.
Saul, it is your David ! Behold ! (*He struggles
to raise the spear vainly, as he strikes a new
attitude.*)

SAUL. It is most memorable—though not
thus do captains usually carry their spears.

DAVID (*troubled*). I know ! (*He has a happy
idea—speaks proudly*) This is my way ! (*The*

H

pride goes from him and he speaks anxiously)
Look—my helmet—if it slips down, then shall
I pass from sight !

> (SAUL *comes to his aid by taking off the
> helmet and*
> DAVID *drags the spear along, leaving it on
> the ground. He looks at* SAUL *affectionately
> and speaks in a puzzled confidential way.
> They are sitting now.*)

King, has it seemed to you that we have something in common, you and I, that we share not
with others ?

SAUL (*surprised*).   Has that come to *you* also ?

DAVID.   A King and a shepherd boy.   How
can it be, Son of Kish ?

SAUL.   Perhaps it is not ordained that you are
always to tend sheep.

DAVID (*confident, smiling at him*).   Foolish
one, things are not ordained about such as
David, but only about kings.

> (SAUL *turns and comes back to him.*)

SAUL.   No thoughts of what may yet come to
pass disturb you, David ?   I would know this.

DAVID.   When I had killed Goliath something
strange did well up in me. (*Shuddering*) Was
it the hereafter, Saul ?

SAUL.   That is what I would know.

DAVID (*uneasily*).   All I have heard about what is to come to pass is of things done by evil spirits and those who call them up.

SAUL (*strongly*).   I, Saul the King, have cut off all such out of this land. (*Huskily*) Nevertheless, one would wish to know. (*Suspiciously*) Said Jonathan anything to you about familiar spirits disquieting me so that a harpist was brought to play before me and drive them away?

DAVID.   No. (*Fearful*) You! Can one playing on a harp do so? (*Lighting up*) Saul, I can play on my harp!

SAUL (*agitated—fiercely*).   They trouble me not. I tell you I have driven them from my kingdom. (*Secretly*) Yet 'tis said there is still one, called the Woman of Endor. (*Huskily*) There are things that kings should know.

DAVID.   Would you foresee that which is to come if you could?

SAUL.   No, no.

DAVID (*breathless*).   I would that I could do so. Have you been to the woman?

SAUL.   Nay, not I. But she has come to me, David, in diverse shapes—even she seemed to be there in this day's battle—warning me not to approach her and yet crooking her finger to entice me. (*Suddenly lowering*) What is it that makes me tell you this ? No others have I told. (*He grips him roughly.*) Now tell me your hidden things. You have them. I know, you crafty one.

DAVID. Crafty ! (*He rises in alarm.*

    SAUL *pulls him down and becomes cunn-*
    ingly reassuring.)

SAUL. Nay, nay. Tell me, David, how did you know about prostrating ?

DAVID (*comfortable again and in his old friendly fashion*). Behold, there was an old man I did see do it.

SAUL. To a king ?

DAVID (*merry at the thought*). No ! (*He tells his cause of merriment.*) Saul, he did it to me !

SAUL (*gripping him*). Be still, boy. This old man—how looked he ?

DAVID. A poor one, but kind. He said he was a prophet.

SAUL. Did he say his name ?

DAVID. He was called Samuel.

    (SAUL *has to take a deep breath before he can*
    speak, but he remains crafty.)

SAUL. Was he ?

DAVID. I do laugh now, but it was not so at the time.

SAUL. Tell me about that time—so that we may laugh together.

DAVID (*who is boyish and confiding*). It was in our house at Bethlehem, and he was secret. He carried a wallet and in it a horn, and he prayed and wetted my head with wet from the horn. And when he was going away he did prostrate himself—before David! (*He laughs at it.*)

(SAUL *controls himself.*)

SAUL. You said he was secret.

DAVID. Yes. Saul, there is some one he fears.

SAUL. There is—and that some one fears him! (*Sharply*) What makes you think that?

DAVID. He said to my mother that if she told the thing he had done there would be but a step between him and me—and Death. King, protect me. (*In a sudden fear he clings to* SAUL.)

SAUL (*pushing him away and holding him at arm's length*). David, how did Samuel kill Goliath?

DAVID (*affronted*). Samuel? That one? It was I killed Goliath.

SAUL. Yours the pebble—but think you Saul can be deceived as are the ignorant? How was it?

DAVID (*letting the admission be drawn out of him*). He only helped.

SAUL. Answer me—who was it?

DAVID. I will not tell you. It was not Samuel. It was—the Other One. Samuel is His servant.

SAUL. At last do I know all. (*He rises and is still kingly, though broken.*) Now am I forsaken.

DAVID (*rising*). You will not tell Jonathan? He thinks I did it all myself. (*Imploring.*)

SAUL (*putting a sorrowful hand on* DAVID'S *head*). Thou doomed boy.

DAVID (*bewildered*). Doomed? Am I doomed, Saul?

SAUL. One of us two friends is doomed.

DAVID (*startled and very child-like*). Do you not like me now?

SAUL (*mournfully*). I like you well. (*He comes to the opening of the tent and, after half-closing it, stands there as if for air.*) David, you should not have told me these things.

(DAVID *has followed him.*)

DAVID (*shrinking*). I know, but I wanted to tell you my things as you have told me yours.

> (SAUL *does not answer, but stands rigid, staring.*
>
> DAVID *gets his harp from back and comes to opening and, sitting on a stool, though still inside the tent like* SAUL, *begins to play. He occasionally looks up, but is mostly looking at his harp. He has no fear of* SAUL.
>
> SAUL *stands much perturbed with one hand on the part of the tent that is still open.*
>
> *The harp music goes on.*)

SAUL (*at last speaking tragically*). There is an enemy in my habitation.

DAVID. An enemy? If it is so, kill him. Saul, kill him! (*He continues to play.*)

SAUL (*after a pause*). I will kill him. David, it is you I am to kill.

DAVID (*looking up and smiling happily*). Oh no, Son of Kish! (*But, seeing* SAUL'S *face, he rises and draws back till he is out of sight, but he never stops playing.*)

> (*For a brief period there is silence except that the harp-playing continues.*
>
> SAUL *is gazing at him, as has been said of*

*the Rembrandt picture, devilish of one eye
and with a tear for* DAVID *in the other.
Then he draws close the remaining part of
the opening.*

*The tent is now shut up. The light con-
tinues to show through the interstices ; and
the harp goes on.*

SAUL *raises one side of the opening of the
tent and throws his javelin. The harp stops
abruptly and the light within the tent goes
out.*

After SAUL *has thrown the javelin at* DAVID
*and the harp has stopped and the light gone
out in the closed tent, he stands a second
listening to the dead silence within the tent.
Then with inarticulate cries, laughter and
wild gestures he sweeps across the stage
triumphant—challenging.*

*Suddenly he stands rigid as though hearing
a voice call,* ' Hast thou slain the Lord's
anointed ? '

*Eyes staring wildly, he shakes with fear.
Then he turns and in a tremulous voice, as
one who calls for help, cries brokenly,*
' David . . . David.'

No sound from within, SAUL, *a doomed*

*figure, with his back to the tent, slowly,
unsteadily sinks down on to a tree-trunk and
buries his head in his arms. After a few
seconds, during which nothing is heard but
the heavy breathing of* SAUL, DAVID'S *head
peeps out of the tent. He is wide-eyed,
bewildered, frightened and very sad.*

At sight of the collapsed SAUL *his first
thoughts are only of immediate flight.
Noiselessly, swift as a wild animal, with his
harp under his arm, he climbs up the rocks
in the background, and is almost safely out
of reach when he suddenly stops and looks
irresolutely at* SAUL. *Something seems to
draw him back to the enemy. Stealthily he
creeps nearer and nearer to* SAUL, *fear, love
and pity in his eyes. Timidly he kneels
down far away from* SAUL, *but keeping
anxious eyes fixed on him.*

*He begins to play his harp—with one hand
only—as though uncertain if this is the
right thing to do.*

SAUL *does not stir.*

Slowly, without ever leaving off playing,
DAVID *creeps on his knees closer and closer.
He begins to play a little more boldly.*

At last SAUL *moves.*

DAVID *holds his breath.*

Then, with great courage and determination, he draws quite close and plays his harp strongly—confidently, but never taking his eyes off SAUL.

Listening, SAUL *slowly raises his head and turns like one returning from another world.*

There is great danger in his expression when he recognises DAVID *crouched, playing at his feet—smiling—radiantly happy.*

Then all tension leaves SAUL *and he is merely listening to the music like one very far away.*)

CURTAIN

ACT III

ACT III

Scene 1

IN A VISION OF THE NIGHT DAVID FORESEES HIS FUTURE, AND KNOWS IT NOT

The Scene is the house of Jesse, as in Act I, except that the time is now late evening. The room is dimly lit by a lamp of the period. The fire is no longer in evidence. It is bed-time and the household of Jesse is about to retire to rest.

In those days the preparations were of the most primitive. The beds were merely mattresses or a skin on the floor, with seldom anything for a pillow, and were huddled together as suited the convenience of the household. There was scarcely any undressing beyond shoes or a coat, and they often added warmer garments instead of taking anything off.

Jesse and David and the four sons of Act I are to sleep here to-night as usual, and certain preparations have already begun. Three of the beds are already on the floor, including David's, which is down-stage.

125

(DAVID *is already in bed, placidly drinking
his evening milk, dipping bread in it and
licking his bowl. He wears a white garment
not unlike a modern nightgown though of
ancient days.*

*The only other person present just now is
his* MOTHER. *This little woman is of in-
exhaustible energy, and has a way of putting
things in their place by butting her head at
them. On rise of Curtain she is climbing
perilously to the window at back, carrying
a board which is its shutter. She has difficulties with it but rams it cleverly in with
one of those butts, just as it was about to fall.
The characteristic of her butts is that she
takes the object suddenly unawares, but
there must be an avoidance of seeming to do
it for stage effect; it is all just part of the
day's work. She finds a big lump in a bed
and plays sudden dab at it with her knees
instead of her head. All this is of the
briefest. She is quick, vital, and an appall-
ingly active housewife, and in a few moments
she is by the side of* DAVID.

*He, being accustomed to her ways, is re-
gardlessly drinking his milk. Having last*

*seen him holding his own in royal company,
we now see him helpless in the hands of this
whirlwind of a woman.*

*All these silent scenes should be brief, with
apparent leisureliness.*)

MOTHER.   Spilt again !   Never did I see such
waste !   (*She whirls him down, wipes him.*)

(*He submits placidly, as he knows he must.*)
(*She surveys him doggedly.*)   Now sleep.   At once !
One, two, three !   He sleeps !   (*Suspiciously ex-
amining him, warningly.*)   He sleeps, I tell you.

DAVID (*quaking*).   Not in the dark !   Mother,
you promised to give me a rush-light.

(*This woman is secretly proud of him now,
but there is no soft sentiment in her.   She is
still hopelessly perplexed about what it all
means.*)

MOTHER.   No more talk of rush-lights.   (*Sitting on his bed.*)   How it comes to be that you
who are afraid to sleep in the dark killed this
Goliath . . . (*despairingly*)—I know not.

DAVID (*who easily loses faith in himself*).   I did
kill him, Mother, didn't I ?

MOTHER (*worried*).   You *say* you did.

DAVID (*faltering*).   When it is light, I know I
did, but in the dark I am not so sure.

MOTHER (*shaking her head*). Nor would I be sure if it were not that we have the spear.

DAVID (*brightening*). Yes! The spear! Is it hid in a new place to-night?

MOTHER (*looking round cautiously*). Hsh! Yes, another new place. (*Scared*) David, when the news spreads to our neighbours, it will do the work of Bethlehem for days untold.

DAVID (*glorious*). My brothers will say we are the eight sons of Jesse!

MOTHER. Hsh! Not a word on your life to anyone until Samuel comes again.

DAVID (*obediently*). No, oh no!

MOTHER. Unless the ass acquires speech we are safe. Yet, though none here knew it was you, reports are already circling round the well of Bethlehem that the giant was killed by some boy. They even say that he cut off Goliath's head.

DAVID. Do they? (*He is promptly possessed by the grandeur of this idea.*) I remember now, I did cut off his head. I sawed it off with the spear!

MOTHER. Thou little liar! (*Troubled*) What am I to think? (*Gazing at* DAVID) How may I believe that a king had the heart to throw a javelin at your yellow head!

DAVID. My shepherd-man ! He did not mean to throw it at me, but at another, who was his enemy ; he was distraught because of that enemy and did mix us up. I do love him still.

MOTHER (*despairingly*). It is beyond me.

DAVID. Mother, I have lost my sling.

MOTHER. Careless boy !

DAVID. The sling I killed Goliath with ! (*He is in despair.*)

MOTHER (*relenting*). Your sling is safe. (*She shows it to him slung secretly round her neck and concealed in her bosom.*)

DAVID (*dumbfounded*). Why have you it there ?

MOTHER (*she becomes harsher, to get away from sentiment*). Sleep, I tell you, you confusion ! And no more of that dreaming of yours and hiding your head beneath the coverlet. Then do you look little like a champion !

DAVID (*quivering*). They were not as dreams, for lo, it was as if they lived.

MOTHER. They ? What mean you by they ?

DAVID (*huskily*). Do you think they are they that Saul spoke of—that which is to come to pass ?

MOTHER (*exasperated*). Some curse was on me

I

when I bore you, boy. (*She treats him roughly and is going off with his bowl when*

    AMNON *enters at back with two nearly empty sacks flung over his shoulders.*)

MOTHER (*she speaks sharply*). You are late again, Amnon. (*Contemptuously*) The maidens at the well, I suppose.

AMNON. Ah me ! (*He is jealous of* DAVID'S *dress and speaks sarcastically*) Are these old eyes mistaken or do they see David in a coat of the night ?

    (DAVID *displays himself vaingloriously.*)

MOTHER. You all had a coat of the night at his years. Moreover, it is the same coat.

    (*She goes out L.*

    AMNON *takes off his shoes, kneads his bed for bumps, finds another bed that he likes better and gets into it, rolling up his sacks as pillows.*

    AMINADAB *and* SHAMMAH *enter L, carrying their beds, and place them ; neither uses a pillow, but both put on warm coats of wool as their one preparation for bed.*

    ELIAB *enters from back in a merry mood— but not at all intoxicated.*

    The MOTHER *returns from L.*)

AMNON. See Eliab roistering, Mother. He has been boasting in the rest-house of his deeds at the camp of Saul.

MOTHER (*tartly*). It is high time that he returned thereto.

ELIAB. Ay, they need me. (*He makes a sort of dancing approach to his bed.*

All are lying down or sitting on their beds when JESSE *enters* L *in his shirt sleeves.*)

JESSE (*heavily*). Woman, I am disturbed about the ass. I notice some change in him. He is less compliant, and brays haughtily as if he thought himself a more notable ass than of old.

MOTHER. Can it be so ?

(*But she and* DAVID *exchange looks of subtle meaning.*

JESSE *is putting on a thick coat.*)

Which bed for you to-night, Jesse ?

JESSE (*yawning*). Let me see. Where is Amnon ?

AMNON. I am here, Father.

JESSE. Arise, Amnon. I will take your bed. Your choice is ever sound.

(AMNON *submits and they all get settled in their beds.*)

MOTHER (*now holding the lamp*).   May good slumber be your hap, Jesse.

JESSE (*as his good-night greeting*).   And yours. But it depends on that David, and his dreams. (*He holds up belt.*) This is for the first who breaks my rest to-night.

> (*The* MOTHER, *after one glance round, goes off L, carrying the lamp.*
>
> *The room is not quite plunged in darkness, as a little light comes from door L, which she has not closed.*
>
> *There is a pause.*)

DAVID.   Father !

JESSE.   Quiet there !

DAVID.   Five minutes, Father ?

JESSE.   No.

DAVID.   Two minutes, Father ?

JESSE.   No.

DAVID.   One minute and a turn-round ?

JESSE.   Belt !

DAVID (*looking up after a pause*).   Is Father asleep, Aminadab ?

AMINADAB.   He is—and so am I.

DAVID.   Eliab, was there more talk at the well about a boy having killed Goliath ?

AMNON (*yawning*).   Eliab sleeps.   But that

story is a foolishness, David—it is more like the sort of thing you do make up yourself.

DAVID (*at once full of misgivings*). Did I make it up, Amnon ?

(*Even* AMNON *is now asleep.*)
Amnon ! (*He is frightened at the stillness and pulls the blanket over his face.*)

(*A brief pause.*

Then the MOTHER *is seen for a second pulling-to the door L, and all is now black darkness.*

Other things unseen by audience have been happening since the darkness came. The back wall of the room has gone. It is really a change of scene without the curtain falling. There is perhaps low music, apparently to introduce the visions, but really to give DAVID *time to change into a man. There is no other music throughout the visions. These visions begin with mysterious clouds and lights passing across the stage and gradually revolving themselves into the first vision. These visions can occupy all the stage from front to back.*

There are in all six of these visions, but as far as possible there should be no pause

*between them; they should pass, slowly
and dreamily, and without any jerks, the
one into the other so that we are as it were
looking upon one continuous picture. This
can best be done, probably, by having no
genuine scenery and the whole affair being
a matter of curtains whose positions can
be got by lighting, etc., as a vague scenic
alteration has to be got from time to time.
A sort of ghostly greyness is perhaps the best
colour, and it should show grey not only in
the curtains but in the clothing and even to
an extent in the faces of the characters, for
it is a suggestion of ghost figures of the
future that we should get. If necessary,
there can be the drifting clouds, etc., after
each vision.*

*Except the words they speak, no sound
should come from these visions—for instance,
we hear no footsteps. There is no furniture
of any kind, unless specifically stated. In
interiors there are no doors, or windows, or
' wings '; the characters are just there or
not there. They come and go by the help of
curtains insubstantially, as if vanishing or
appearing from a mist. All this calls for*

*adroitness from stage experts that is beyond
the author's skill, who knows what he wants
but not how to get it and has now given them
enough to ponder over for one day. With
a big stage, some of the scenes should attain
a grandeur of effect.*

*The first vision shows the Cave of Adullam.
It is a vague place with an opening at the
back and rocks in it, made no doubt of
velvet. The general effect of it should be
wild, and here and elsewhere in the visions
when they are out of doors, they should be
reproductions of ancient places.*

*Several Israelite soldiers, armed, appear
among the rocks, evidently in search of
DAVID. They come without a sound,
tracking him. They see indications that
there has been a fire and draw their swords.
The scene should be dim. OPHIR and
ABNER are in command of these men.)*

OPHIR.   Search the glade beyond. Tell them to
put a ring of searchers round this and every cave.

ABNER.   If you would be live men in the
morning.   For so Saul swears.

*(Only OPHIR and ABNER are now left. They
crouch down by the fire.)*

ABNER.   Truly there are evil shadows flitting through these caves to-night.

OPHIR.   We seek but one of them—the son of Jesse.

ABNER.   But again and again he avoids out of our presence.   He is as one protected against such as Ophir and Abner.

OPHIR.   But not against such a one as Saul.

ABNER.   Saul has made the mountains drunk with the blood of his enemies.   But still David escapes him.   So seems it to be again to-night.

(*In the opening at the back* SAUL *suddenly appears.*)

SAUL (*fiercely*).   You have not found mine enemy ?

OPHIR.   Every cave on the mountain is being searched.   We know by this fire that he was hiding here within the hour.

SAUL.   Ever within the hour !   What is this place called ?

OPHIR.   It is known as the Cave of Adullam.

ABNER.   We had hoped that the priests of the place called Nob would guide you to him.

SAUL (*savagely*).   There is now no place called Nob.

OPHIR.   But the priests of Nob.

SAUL. There are no longer priests in Nob.

ABNER (*aghast*). You cannot mean that——

SAUL. When they refused to lead me to him I ordered my servants to smite them to the wall.

ABNER. My King! Priests!

SAUL. Ay, so my servants cried and would not put forth their hands, but Doeg the Edomite was faithful and fell upon the priests, and four score and five who wore the linen ephod did he slay.

ABNER (*horrified*). Sacrilege!

SAUL. To that have I come.

OPHIR. It was but excess of zeal.

SAUL. The same zeal shall be apportioned to you—and you—if David is not delivered into my hands. If again we fail I shall do as I have spoken of to you, Ophir! I will make him my son-in-law so that my daughter may snare him.

OPHIR. Not that, O King!

> (*The second vision, which requires a much larger space of stage, shows* SAUL *and his troop asleep on a hillside. His head is on a sort of kit-bag called a ' bolster,' and his javelin stands erect by him, stuck in the ground.*

Near him lies OPHIR, *and both are prominent down-stage.*

The other sleeping figures are more vague. It is a bright clear night.

DAVID *appears at top on the hillside and we realise that his object is to reach* SAUL, *a very dangerous venture. Dagger in hand, ready to stab anyone who wakes, he descends, stepping over bodies. He reaches the side of the King. He is conscious of his remarkable position beside his enemy. He raises his dagger threateningly and pauses, indicating how easy it would be to do the deed. Then he proceeds to mysterious, dangerous business, holding his dagger in his teeth. He pulls the bolster inch by inch from beneath* SAUL's *head. Once* SAUL *moans a little and* DAVID *holds the dagger ready to strike. Having got the bolster, he takes out of it a leather cruse of water. He also wants* SAUL's *javelin, but* OPHIR's *hand is on it. Pulling a hair from his own head, he tickles* OPHIR's *hand with it, ready to kill if he wakes.* OPHIR *does not wake, but merely removes his hand, scratches it, and sleeps on.*

DAVID *pulls the javelin out of the ground and, carrying it and the water cruse, he goes up the incline across the bodies. He stops and lays them down and, looking among the bodies for something, finds it. It is a horn. He pulls a hand across his brow, implying that now he has reached the riskiest moment of his schemes. Then he boldly sounds the horn—that is, though we hear no sound, the action implies this. Possibly this one sound should be heard.*

As if the sleepers had heard it, the horn wakens the SOLDIERS *and they answer with cries and grasp their weapons.*

DAVID *is now standing, a conspicuous figure, surrounded by soldiers ready to pounce on him, his arms folded.*

SAUL *and* OPHIR *start up, and* ABNER *and others pointing at* DAVID *add to his prominence.*)

OPHIR (*pointing*). My King, your enemy!

ABNER. Behold we deliver him into your hands.

DAVID (*speaking for the first time in the visions*). *You* deliver me, Abner, son of Ner! Asleep all of you, dastards, at your posts! What opportunity this night for men of evil intent to have crept over your vile bodies and slain the Lord's anointed !

SAUL.   He speaks true.   Abner, Ophir, you are both worthy of death.

OPHIR.   His words are false, O King.   Never were guards more watchful.   He knows he could not have come one step nearer you and lived.

DAVID.   I have wandered through you and over you and stood by the side of the King.

SAUL.   Nay, nay, that cannot have been, for I still live.

OPHIR.   Not once did I close an eye, and my hand never failed to clutch thy javelin.

SAUL (*to* DAVID).   Thou hearest ?

DAVID.   Where, then, my Ophir, is the javelin that your hand never failed to clutch ?

(*Consternation when they find it has gone.*)

DAVID.   Where, O King, is the cruse of water that was in the bolster on which you thought the head of Saul lay safe ?

(*They find that it also has gone ; increased astonishment.*

DAVID *holds up, one in each hand, the cruse and the javelin.*

There are cries of wonder.)

Now let one of the young men come up and fetch the King's javelin and the cruse that was in his bolster.

(*This is done.*)

OPHIR (*contrite*). My King! (*His arms seek forgiveness, but*

SAUL *strikes them down.*)

SAUL. Unworthy!

DAVID. Behold, Saul, I have taught these slovens that they should be a wall unto you by night and by day. Yet you have driven me from your service and hunted me through all Judah, seeking my life, and you came hither to tear it out of me on this mountain of the he-goats. You have chased me into serving other Lords whom I loved less than thee but trusted more. Now am I in thy grasp. Slay me as I stand if such is still your wish. Your young men's daggers are around me, and even Ophir and Abner are at last awake.

SAUL. Thou art bold of speech. Yet, my son David, I will no more do thee harm nor seek to pursue thee into the bowels of the earth or to snare thee like a pheasant on the mountains, but I will take thee back into my service because my soul was precious in thine eyes this night.

(DAVID *prostrates himself and the scene changes into a vague interior in the palace of Saul. There are no doors or windows to it. It is only an empty space with curtains but it has one piece of furniture, namely a throne raised on two steps, and on the throne is sitting* SAUL *in kingly garments and with the crown on his head.*

OPHIR *appears out of the nothingness.*)

SAUL.   Well ?

OPHIR.   My King, he has made the mountains drunk with the blood of thine enemies.

SAUL (*apprehensive*).   The son of Jesse ?

OPHIR.   The congregation of the people cry that we owe the day to him. They are singing and dancing to his glory in the streets to the music of flute, hackbut, cornet and dulcimer.

SAUL (*dolefully*).   Ophir, it must be done— that of which I spoke to you. (OPHIR *is reluctant.*)

SAUL.   It is the one way of breaking him that has not yet been tried. You spoke to him ?

OPHIR (*miserably*).   I gave him your words. I said : ' Come you now, before the King, for Saul has delight in you.'

SAUL.   Delight !   How looked he at that ?

OPHIR.   He *eyed* me, O King.

SAUL.   Summon me my daughters.

> (OPHIR *fades out, and in the same gradual
> way* MERAB *and* MICHAL, *two beautiful
> young women, daughters of* SAUL, *appear.
> They are finely attired, and* MICHAL *is
> apparently high-spirited.*)

Merab——

> (*She makes a sweeping obeisance.*)

Michal——

> (*She does so also.*)

I have called you before the throne because I
have a design to make one of you a snare unto
the son of Jesse.

MERAB.   A snare.   Which one of us ?

SAUL (*sternly*).   Gainsay me not.

> (DAVID *appears.   He is now handsomely
> attired as a captain, and is respectful but
> wary, and prepared for even an attempt upon
> his life.   He makes obeisance.*)

SAUL.   Rise, my captain.   The throne-room
greets you.

DAVID.   O King, I am dazed by it.   Never
have these eyes beheld the throne until this
day.

SAUL. Great has been your victory and I would reward you in a kingly way.

(*The* TWO GIRLS *exchange puzzled glances.*)
This day shall you be my son-in-law.

(DAVID *bows but is still alert.*)

MERAB. Father, which of us?

SAUL (*to* DAVID). Determine it between you.

(*He moves away and is suddenly gone.*)

MERAB (*to* DAVID, *humbling herself before him*). Noble captain, your fame grows apace. You will be too great for me. I am for the simple Adriel.

MICHAL (*remaining erect*). Never, captain, can you be great enough for me. I am for a King.

> (*They see* DAVID *is staring at the throne with such interest that he is oblivious of their presence. They look at each other bewildered and, moving away, they are gone.*
>
> DAVID *is unconscious of their going, and, drawn by something within him, he slowly moves forward and mounts the throne.* MICHAL *now returns softly and watches him from curtain, half in hiding. Perhaps we only see her face.* DAVID *sits on the throne and we see that he likes it.*)

MICHAL (*in an intense murmur and holding out her arms*). I am for a King!

(*She withdraws into the background.*
She goes.

DAVID, *left alone, still sits upon the throne,
no longer fearfully but quite complacently.
Suddenly he claps his hand to his forehead
as if hit by something. He leaves the throne
quickly, bewildered and as one who has done
sacrilege.*

The scene changes to SAUL'S *tent on the
night before the battle of Gilboa.*

SAUL *in armour is pacing the tent, raging
at the shrinking* OPHIR *who is also armed.
Evidently* OPHIR *has brought bad news.
Though* SAUL *rages at first he is now less
spirited than formerly ; he is a more sad-
dened man.*)

SAUL (*fiercely*). Again he has escaped me !
Sent I not you, with messengers, to compass his
house and bring him up to me on his sick-bed
that I may slay him ?

OPHIR (*at his heaviest, as one telling an astound-
ing thing*). Lo, when we were come in to where
he lay there was an image on the bed, with a
pillow of goat's hair for his bolster !—and it was
Michal his wife who did this thing, and let him
down from the window in a basket !

K

SAUL (*bitterly*).   Michal, the child of my bowels whom I had given to him to entice and to snare him !   Even his wife is on the side of this man. What murmur my soldiers against me because I drove him forth from the army of Israel ?

(OPHIR *hesitates*.)

The truth, Ophir.

OPHIR (*reluctantly*).   Your Elders do proclaim that he was the wisest of your counsellors—and your Captains lament that you will not have him in to-morrow's battle, speaking of him as one who breaks upon an enemy like the breach of waters.

SAUL.   And what says Ophir ?

OPHIR (*violently*).   Ophir says he is the falsest in all Israel.

SAUL (*firmly though sadly*).   So says not Saul. Mine enemy has ever fought me fair, and twice had he my life in his hands and returned it to me who slew four score and five of the priests of Nob because they would not deliver him unto me.   I did wickedness that day. (*He shudders at himself*.)   What say my people ?

(OPHIR *hesitates*.)

(*Harshly*) Answer me.

OPHIR.   The more ignorant among the people

cry : 'Saul has slain his thousands but David will slay his tens of thousands.'

SAUL. Ophir, I heard them ! And they were the bitterest words of all to me ! O fickle people ! Will this man give every one of you vines and fig-trees to sit under when the day's toil is done, as I have striven to do ? (*Honourably*) Ay, Ophir, he will, for I have that within me which knows he too does love the people. This man will make the earth shake and tremble, for he is a greater one than Saul. And now there is none of you sorry for me, no not one.

OPHIR. My King ! (*On his knees to* SAUL.)
    (SAUL, *who has been seated, rises and speaks*
    quietly but with resolution.)

SAUL. How long must I drag this chain of life—how long ? Now shall I seek Samuel, and know how long.

OPHIR (*startled*). My King, you know that Samuel's days are fulfilled and that he sleeps with his fathers at Ramah.

SAUL (*firmly*). I go to seek one who can bring him up.

OPHIR (*horrified*). Not the Woman of Endor ! (*Trembling*) King, it is impious to seek to bring up the dead.

SAUL. Leave me, Ophir, in the hour of my strait with the burden that is upon me. And hearken. Everyone now to his tent. I must be alone in this world to-night.

(OPHIR *goes.*

SAUL *is left alone. After shivering once, he is firm of purpose. He peers out of the tent. The scene is now the cavern of the* WITCH OF ENDOR. *It should be specially vague and indeterminate, little more than blackness through which the ancient witch flits and is gone.*

SAUL *appears in disguise. In the tent we have seen him a broken sorrowful man, but now he is of a noble and kingly bearing. He and the* WITCH *meet, but in such darkness that we see only their shapes.*)

SAUL (*as she shrinks back*). You know me not, I am not as you think. I am of this world. Divine unto me by the familiar spirit, and bring him up to me, the one whom I shall name unto thee.

(*The voices of both are pitched in a key to go with the solemnity of the occasion.*)

WITCH (*trembling*). Thou knowest what Saul has done. He has cut off those that have

familiar spirits. Wherefore then layest thou a
snare for my life to cause me to die ?

SAUL.   There shall no punishment happen to
thee for this thing.

WITCH (*whose fears are in contrast to his firmness*). Whom shall I bring up unto thee ?

SAUL.   Bring me up Samuel.

   (*There is suddenly a torch in her hand and
   she is using it to peer at his face.*)

WITCH (*huskily*).   Thou art Saul !

SAUL.   Fear not. What see'st thou ?

WITCH.   An old man cometh up and he is
covered with a mantle.

   (*She vanishes.*

   Perhaps we see less the figure of SAMUEL
   *than a thickness, and we know that someone
   is there.*

   To that SAUL *addresses himself.*)

SAUL.   Samuel ! (*He bows low to the unseen.*)

SAMUEL (*sternly*).   Why hast thou disquieted
me, Saul, to bring me up ?

SAUL (*firm*).   I am sore distressed, for the
Philistines make war against me, and the Lord
answereth me no more. Therefore I have called
thee up that thou mayest make known to me
how long is my time—how long.

SAMUEL (*relentless*). The Lord is departed
from thee, for He rends the kingdom out of thy
hand and gives it to thy neighbour. Because
thou disobeyed'st Him He has done this thing
unto thee. To-morrow, after the battle with the
Philistines, thou and thy son shall no longer be
of this world : you will be in mine with me.

> (SAUL *has listened without flinching. He
> again bows lowly. He sways.*
> *The thickening fades.*
> *The scene dissolves and changes to a moun-
> tain side on the next day, where the Phil-
> istines gained their only great victory over
> the Israelites and* SAUL *was slain. There
> is doubt as to the exact site, but Mount
> Gilboa comes into the picture and the battle
> might be called after it. The Israelites,
> who always chose the higher ground because
> they were without horses or chariots, were
> driven upward and dispersed with great
> slaughter, but all we see is a last effort of*
> SAUL'S *after the fight has been lost. In the
> background many dead of both sides lie,
> seen vaguely as in mist.*
> *In the foreground,* SAUL, *badly wounded,
> is hewing down some of the enemy in the*

*manner of a mighty warrior of old ; but
still we hear no sound. When they are
killed or driven off, he falls, shot by an
arrow.*

OPHIR, *equally wounded, is by him.*

SAUL *in the Old Testament was wearing
his crown.*)

SAUL.   Tell me, is it so with Jonathan—also ?

OPHIR.   Alas ! (*He bows his head.*)

SAUL.   Ophir, truly am I sore wounded by the
archers. Dispatch me now quickly. Thrust me
through, lest the uncircumcised Philistines come
and abuse me.

OPHIR.   I cannot lift my hand against my
King.

SAUL.   I forgive you, sweet Ophir.

(*He dies by his own hand and
OPHIR falls back among the slain.
A figure appears on the battlefield and
resolves himself into the man* DAVID. *He
comes down to the side of* SAUL, *kneels,
then rises and salutes him. He is again
in military rags, as in the second of the
visions.*)

DAVID.   How are the mighty fallen ! Tell it
not in Gath ; publish it not in the streets of

Ascalon, lest the daughters of the Philistines rejoice. Ye mountains of Gilboa, let there be no dew, neither let there be rain, upon you, nor fields of offerings; for here the shield of the mighty is vilely cast away, the shield of Saul, as though he had not been anointed with oil. From the blood of the slain, from the fat of the mighty, the bow of Jonathan turned not back, and the sword of Saul returned not empty. Saul and Jonathan were lovely and pleasant in their lives, and in their death they were not divided; they were swifter than eagles, they were stronger than lions. Ye daughters of Israel, weep over Saul who clothed you in scarlet, with other delights. (*Now addressing a body which we do not distinguish*) O Jonathan, thou wast slain in thine high places. I am distressed for thee, my brother Jonathan; very pleasant hast thou been unto me; thy love to me was wonderful, passing the love of women. How are the mighty fallen, and the weapons of war perished! (*He sinks down, mourning for* JONATHAN, *and is gone.*)

> (*The figure of* SAMUEL *comes to* SAUL. *Throughout the scene that follows they are as simple as two villagers gossiping about old times.*)

SAMUEL.   Greeting, friend.   Can I help you ?
     (SAUL *sits up.*)

SAUL.   Do I know you ?

SAMUEL.   I was called Samuel.

SAUL.   I cannot remember such a one, but I like your face.

SAMUEL.   And I yours—though it is unknown to me.

SAUL.   Sit with me, good Samuel.
     (SAMUEL *sits beside him.*)

SAMUEL (*uncertain*).   If your name should be Saul——

SAUL.   It comes to me that such is my name.

SAMUEL.   Then, to guide you, I was sent hither, as one who in a past time had, in some way now forgotten by me, been tied up with you in the bundle of life.

SAUL.   Is it so ?   (*Dropping unconsciously into* DAVID's *manner*) Now do you ask me what was my way of life, and I will tell you, and then shall I ask you what was your way of life, and, lo, you will tell me.   (*Puzzled*) Was it you who used to say this to me ?

SAMUEL.   I know not.   But tell me, Saul, what was your way of life ?

SAUL.   I was a shepherd.   Now tell me what was yours.

SAMUEL.   I see it not so clearly as you do, for I am farther away.   All I bring back is that I had two troublesome sons.   How one forgets the smaller things !

SAUL.   Verily.

SAMUEL (*ruminating*).   A shepherd ?   It is as if I had known such a one—one who went out into far places to seek his asses which had strayed.

SAUL.   Not my asses, my father's asses.

SAMUEL.   It was you ?

SAUL.   One forgets not such a thing as that.

SAMUEL (*his memory jogged*).   Tell me, were you never a King ?

SAUL.   What is that ?

SAMUEL.   One who is lord-over-all.

SAUL (*quietly reproving*).   Speak not blasphemy, friend.   There is but One such.

SAMUEL.   It is so.   Nevertheless——

   (*He prostrates before* SAUL, *whom it vaguely disturbs.*)

SAUL.   What mean you ?   Trouble me not.

SAMUEL.   Thus did all your people.

SAUL.   Who were my people ?

SAMUEL.   They were called Israel.

SAUL.   Israel. It is a beautiful word.

SAMUEL.   Put all such vanity from you, friend.

SAUL.   What happened, Samuel ? Was the Lord fair to me ? (*Giving it up contentedly*) Truly His ways are past finding out.

SAMUEL.   Now are they to be made clear to you. Come with me.

SAUL.   Israel.

> (*They go away together.*
> *The scene darkens, and in the obscurity of the battlefield, we become aware of a small white figure wandering about on it. Only the white nightgown makes us realise that this is the boy* DAVID. *He is flitting about here and there, in search of* SAUL, *but does not find him. He calls :*)

Saul—Saul !

> (*After a pause :*)

It is thy David seeking thee !

> (*Again, after a pause :*)

Shepherd !

> (*Finally :*)

Saul, Saul !

> (*His childishness is in strong contrast to the virility of the older* DAVID.

The scene blacks out, and changes to the room of the sleepers, the back wall being replaced, and they are still lying there asleep.

It should be noted that all sounds made in the room are now heard though none were heard in the visions.

The room is still dark, but, as the MOTHER *enters L, the grey light of early morning comes through the doorway which she has left open. It is now lighter in the room but only light enough to show the sleeping figures. The* MOTHER *is evidently the first up to meet the labours of the new day, and is carrying a broom. She comes to* DAVID'S *bed, expecting all to be as usual, and is startled to find that he is not in the bed. This should be unexpected to us also. She utters one alarmed cry :)*

MOTHER.   Jesse !

(And then realises that it is best not to waken the others. While she is pondering what to do, the back door opens and DAVID *comes in, still wearing his white garment, which is now bedraggled. He leaves the door open, which adds to the amount of light. His*

eyes are glassy and he moves like a sleep-walker. She murmurs his name, and she both goes to him and shrinks back, for she has a feeling that in his condition he ought not to be addressed.

He does not see her, though she is in full view, but goes straight to his bed and lies on it like a log, in an extremity of sleep and exhaustion.

She is no longer emotional. She is entirely practical. She takes off her shawl and puts it round his shoulders. She is startled to find his sling round his waist. She feels her own neck, thinking it is surely still there. She looks at door L as a suspicion comes to her.)

MOTHER (*bewildered*). Your sling! Did you come in to where I lay and take it off me while I slept? (*She finds his knee cut and bandages it. She says in awe:*) David, where have you been?

(*He sleeps on.*)

End of Scene 1

SCENE 2

DAVID AND JONATHAN

The Scene, which is pastoral, is the fields south-east of Bethlehem, and here David is found tending his sheep. It is early evening two days later and the setting sun lingers over its best achievement. We may see a suggestion of its rays, but not the sun itself. It should be an idyll of quiet rural loveliness, in contrast to the rest of the play. In the not far distance is the old walled town of Bethlehem on its hill, not conspicuous and yet vaguely dominating the landscape, which shows many of the wild flowers for which this place was famous, such as the white flower called the Star of Bethlehem, with masses of scarlet anemones. A half-cut field of barley is also prominent, shining at times in the sun. In the foreground, near C but not centre, is a large rock (practical) of limestone which slopes from R to L, beginning from ground and reaching at its highest point to nearly five feet. Thus it is really a small rock, though to David's eyes it is great. It extends back sufficiently far to contain a small cave just large enough to hold two people. It has moss growing on it, and there are similar

*smaller rocks here and there going into distance,
for it is not rich ground for pasture but often stony.
In the foreground down-stage R there is a thick
patch of long grass (practical), about half a dozen
yards of it.*

*All the action of this scene of country life must
take place down-stage. It really consists of a
duologue between the two boys, and must not play
much more than ten minutes. There are possibly
some real sheep and black goats browsing here and
there, but in any case most of them are artificial.
There are bells round their necks, and at the opening
of the scene (before any talk) the tinkle of the bells
is heard, but this must not be over-done. It should
be no louder than the hum of bees.*

　　　　(DAVID *is discovered standing on the rock
　　　　crest tending his sheep. A shepherd's staff
　　　　with crooked handle is in his hand and it is
　　　　much taller than himself ; he has to reach
　　　　to grasp the handle. He is wearing a long
　　　　shepherd's mantle of linen, no doubt stitched
　　　　together by his mother, though he thinks he
　　　　is looking every inch a shepherd, and he
　　　　should have the effect of a shepherd as seen
　　　　in the pictures of the period.*

*His hand is outstretched and he seems to
be numbering the sheep. Seeing that all is
well with his flock,* DAVID *sits on the rock
pursuing a secret occupation. He has now
a lump of soft clay in his hand on which he
is laboriously writing a letter. This is done
with a sharp instrument in his knife, and is
really carving. His head is cocked in the
effort and he is biting his tongue. The peace-
ful pastoral scene is interrupted by someone
unseen throwing clods of earth at him. He
evidently guesses who it is and he jumps
down and hides in his cave.*

A whistle is heard off-stage. DAVID
whistles back and hides in cave.

The voice of JONATHAN *calls :)*

JONATHAN.   Son of Jesse !

(DAVID *thinks it all exceedingly funny.*

JONATHAN *enters, not in armour, but well
attired. He sees* DAVID *but politely pre-
tends not to.)*

David ! Whither have you got ? I saw you on
the rock like a he-goat.

DAVID (*like sentry*).   Say the password.

JONATHAN.   Goliath.

DAVID.   Enter !

(JONATHAN *affects surprise to see him.*
DAVID *and he point at each other gleefully.*
DAVID *emerges on all fours. He winces and
limps and sits down on the ground.*)

JONATHAN.   Have you hurt yourself?

DAVID (*emphatic*).   No!

(JONATHAN *sits beside him.*)

(DAVID *pulls bandage off his knee and shows
bandage dramatically*) Behold! (*He then shows
his knee badly scratched.*)

JONATHAN.   How then?   Have more strange
things befallen *you* who killed Goliath but two
days ago?

DAVID.   Ay, truly!   (*Impressively*) Jonathan,
hearken.   My mother says I did wander from my
home in the dark of the night, and whither I
went no one knows!   (*He is rather scared.*)
Jonathan, have you ever been at a dream?

JONATHAN.   At a dream?   I have dreamed
dreams, but you cannot be *at* a dream.

DAVID (*complacently, but uncomfortable*).   *I*
can!

JONATHAN.   You are sure?

DAVID.   My mother is sure.   When she sought
me on my bed in the morning, I was not there,
and then did I come in by the door and I saw her

L

not, for my eyes were glassy. But my sling was in my hand and this knee did bleed, and she plucked from it thorns of the field. Jonathan, I had been at a dream !

JONATHAN (*awed*). You are a strange one, David.

DAVID (*also awed but pleased*). Am I not ?

JONATHAN. Show me your dream.

DAVID. It has now gone from me.

JONATHAN. Thus is it with dreams. (*With boyish eagerness*) Was I in it ?

DAVID (*reflecting*). I do not remember you in it.

JONATHAN. Then it interests me not.

DAVID. I think your father was in it.

JONATHAN. Tell me.

DAVID. Something about Saul and an enemy. (*Puzzled*) What enemy ? (*With excited glimpses of memory*) He was a ragged soldier seeking the hurt of Saul, and so I rose from my bed and went out with my sling to kill him. (*Realising*) Ay, that was why I went out into the dream.

JONATHAN. I am happy, David, that you do so love my father even in dreams.

DAVID. Also I do love you.

JONATHAN. And I you.

DAVID.   Jonathan, I have made a gift for you.

JONATHAN.   What is it ?

(DAVID *gets on to rock and lifts the lump of clay, covering it with his hand as a treasure.* JONATHAN *eagerly jumps up beside him and tries to open the hands of* DAVID. *They are sitting on rock.*)

DAVID (*putting it into* JONATHAN'S *hand*).   Now is it yours. Nay, be careful—it is now but soft clay, but when it is baked in the sun it will be . . . a brick !

JONATHAN.   Only a brick ! (*disappointed but polite*).   Truly a comely brick.

DAVID (*trying not to be lordly*).   Jonathan, it is a letter !

(JONATHAN *examines it with wonder.*)

JONATHAN.   You can write ?

DAVID (*swelling*).   Behold ! (*Pointing to it.*)

JONATHAN.   I cannot write.   It is not for princes to practise such things.

(DAVID *offers it to him.*)

JONATHAN.   Nor do we read.   (*Eagerly*) How speaks it ?

DAVID.   It says : ' I, David, son of Jesse, am the one who slew Goliath, and none helped me, for I did it alone.' Thus, Jonathan, will my

sons know 'twas I and no other who did it, and
their sons and theirs and theirs down to for ever
and a span will know, for such can be the life of
a brick with writing on it.

JONATHAN. O excellent brick. (*Regally*) David,
when I am King I will make you one of my
guard.

DAVID.   No, Jonathan, I have slain a lion and
a bear and now is my great day ended.

JONATHAN.   All things shall be as I direct.
Sometimes you shall sit at my table.

DAVID.   In my dream I saw the ragged one
sit upon a throne.

JONATHAN.   Was he anyone you know ?

DAVID.   No, he was a bad one. I can remember no more.

(JONATHAN *shivers*.)

JONATHAN.   He sat upon a throne ? David,
I like not this.

DAVID.   Then did I loose a pebble at him—
and it struck him in the brow. Quickly did he
leap from that throne ! There was also a woman
in the dream (*sadly, as if this were a phrase of
portentous meaning*) and, alas, she was fair to look
upon. I think she was his wife, and he did call
her Michal. . . . Here is another thing I do re-

member now. When he was old, he cried : ' O my son Absalom ! Would that I had died for thee, O Absalom, my son, my son ! ' That time was I sorry for him—and I did vow never to call a son of mine Absalom.

(Dismissing the dream.)

Jonathan, come into my cave so that I may propose a hidden thing to you.

(They sit in the cave. DAVID *speaks rapturously.)*

Jonathan, shall you and I make a covenant ?

JONATHAN *(in the same spirit).* Let us ! But what ?

(They are gleeful again.)

DAVID. To be friends for ever and ever and a span !

JONATHAN. Whatever thy soul desireth, that will I do for thee, David.

DAVID. And so I swear I will do for thee. Behold now we have sworn.

JONATHAN. So we have ! Now, David, show me how you killed the lion and the bear.

DAVID. I will show you. Stand there and be the lion and I will come out of my cave and kill you. *(He goes into the cave.* JONATHAN *gets ready to play the part of the lion. David comes out of the cave and attacks* JONATHAN. *After a short fight* JONATHAN *throws* DAVID *to the ground.* DAVID *is bewildered.* JONATHAN, *very pleased with himself, laughs loudly.*)

DAVID.　How shall I be able to kill you unless you roar ?　Try again, foolish one. (*He goes back into the cave.* JONATHAN *roars.* DAVID *rushes at him and, after a short struggle, he is thrown again.* JONATHAN *laughs.*)

JONATHAN.　Now shall I be the bear ?

DAVID.　Never, never, never ! (*He fetches brick and throws it down, battering it to pieces.*) Begone, thou lying brick !

JONATHAN (*bewildered*).　Lying ?

DAVID (*now reaching the most tragic moment in his boyhood's story*).　I wrote on my brick that I alone killed Goliath and that none helped me ; and that is false ; for *He* helped me !

JONATHAN (*completely at sea*).　He ?　Who ? David, these eyes saw your pebble that pierced the giant between the eyes.

DAVID.　It was His pebble.

JONATHAN.　Whose ?

　　　(*After a moment* DAVID *whispers the terrible secret in his ear.*

When JONATHAN, *who has looked upward, is able to speak, he says shakily :)*

Oh, David! Are you not then so wonderful as I thought ?

DAVID (*mournfully*). No.

JONATHAN. But you did slay a lion and a bear, didn't you ?

DAVID (*in bitter humiliation*). 'Twas also He who slew the lion and the bear.

JONATHAN (*slightly drawing away from him*). Oh, David! (*Eager to comfort*) But He let you help ?

DAVID (*in despair*). He did not need my help. (*With a cry*) I want to do something all by myself!

JONATHAN. Oh, David. Only kings can do things by themselves.

(DAVID *is sad for a moment.*)

Now must I seek the camp.

DAVID. And I my home. (*He lifts the staff.*) But first I must go round my fold and separate the sheep from the goats.

(*The dying sun is now bright over the scene, especially over the barley field.*)

JONATHAN. It is fair to look upon around Bethlehem.

DAVID. There is no place so fair as Bethlehem. So did Naomi think—and Ruth.

JONATHAN. Who were they ?

DAVID. Naomi was of Bethlehem, and when she was old she did always want to come back here from a far land where she was wed. And Ruth was her daughter-in-law and said to her : ' Whither thou goest I will go, and where thou lodgest I will lodge : thy people shall be my people, and thy God my God, and where thou diest will I die, and there will I be buried '—and so, Jonathan, did it come to pass. But first she did glean in the field, for it was the time of the barley ; but the man Boaz did tell the reapers slyly to let fall handfuls so that she should get more than her share ! And thus did she wed Boaz, and became the mother of Obed, who begat Jesse, who begat me ! (*Pointing*) And that is the field in which he first saw her, and lo, it is again the time of the barley !

JONATHAN. The day groweth to an end. Whistle to me as I go David, our whistle.

DAVID (*lying on his back*). None will harm you as you go, for those you may meet will be but poor shepherds that do lie in fields keeping their flocks by night. Such shall I

be, Jonathan, through all the nights of my
life.

JONATHAN (*he lifts the two biggest pieces of clay*).
Alas, once proud brick.

DAVID (*taking them and dropping them in little
pieces*). Its day has been shorter than we
thought! (*Swelling*) Nevertheless, I have still
Goliath's spear.

JONATHAN. When you are a man, David, I
will see to it that you carry that spear on your
shoulder.

DAVID (*whispering*). Jonathan, *I can carry it
on my shoulder now!*

JONATHAN. Not you! Is that the secret?
(DAVID *nods.*)

DAVID. Jonathan, it is something I did
think out by myself. (*With a half-defiant,
half-apprehensive look upwards*) None helped
me.

JONATHAN. Show me.

DAVID. Some day I will show you.

JONATHAN. Now am I gone. (*He starts to go,
then turns and puts his hand on* DAVID'S *shoulder.*)
Remember the covenant. David and Jonathan
friends for ever.

DAVID. And a span!

(*They are not sentimental. They are gay and happy.*

JONATHAN *goes off the way he had come.*

In the same moment DAVID *gets on the rock, to look after him.*

JONATHAN *does the whistle, unseen.*

DAVID, *staff in hand, on the rock, whistles it. They whistle to each other till* JONATHAN *is too far away.*

DAVID *comes off the rock. He leaves his staff in the cave. He is sly and has some grand design on hand. He drags into view by both hands Goliath's spear, which so far has been hidden in the long grass in front. He drags it along the ground and up the sloping rock. Then, standing where the rock is highest, he pulls the spear on to him till it is balanced on his shoulder.*

With one glance upwards he goes off elatedly L, with the spear over his shoulder. There is a slight accompaniment of sheep-bells.)

THE END